Making
Vanilla Extract
~Expert Level~

℘

This awesome book includes:

- ◆ Bean to Alcohol Calculation Sheets
- ◆ Batch Logs, Diary and Batch P&L
- ◆ How to Dilute your Everclear and step by step Dilution Calculations
- ◆ Beans and Supplies suggestions and sources
- ◆ Several Recipe's from basic to unique
- ◆ Cottage Industry Information & Labeling
- ◆ And so much more!

Table of Contents

Chapter 1
What Goes Into Making Great Vanilla

Introduction

❧

Vanilla, the pods from a member of the orchid family, were originally grown in South and Central America, and the Caribbean. It's production has since spread to many corners of the world but the best most flavorful producers of Vanilla by far are in the Sava district of Madagascar. "More than half the global vanilla production comes from this region. Despite the heavy workload and thriving vanilla economy, some Vanilla farmers can barely survive off the land. Madagascar is one of the worlds poorest countries and the people who grow this amazing spice are abused and neglected. If you would like to donate this year to a charity – please consider one of the many charities that help these people. But I digress.....

Vanilla, as we all know is a spice used in foods, and beverages, a medicinal drink for stomach ache, (ginger is better) and a scent in perfumes among other things.

Photo's Courtesy the Madagascar Vanilla Company
https://www.madagascarvanillacompany.com/buymadagascarvanillabeans/#sava

The Beans

CB

There are many different types of Beans you can buy to make you vanilla and no end to the amount of companies and middle men that can get their hands and their wallets involved. As it is, Vanilla Bean prices are astronomical, so to get the best price you need to eliminate as many middle men as possible. I've added links in the Sourcing section to help you find reputable companies that sell amazing beans at fair prices. Please visit each of the sites, call and ask questions, and see for yourself what they have to offer.

Lets explore the many different types of beans available to you, which are the best for making extracts and which should never be used. We will also discuss places that overcharge, co-ops, and more. If nothing else, please learn as much as you can about Vanilla Beans so that you are never over charged by middlemen. I saw a company today listing Vanilla beans (no national origin listed) for $580 a pound. That is highway robbery!

Madagascar or Bourbon Vanilla (Planifolia Andrews)

Is the same Bean that's grown in several countries. Madagascar's beans are called "Bourbon" but do not contain Bourbon. These beans are named loosely after the Island Reunion (once known as Bourbon) and the slave who successfully hand pollinated the beans. Sadly there is no actual Bourbon used in growing the beans but that does not mean it can't be used in making the Vanilla.

Madagascar Bourbon Beans are on the thinner side when compared to any of the other popular Vanilla beans. Madagascar Vanilla flavor notes tend to run sweeter and creamier and have been considered the upper echelon of Vanilla Beans. These beans come in a flat and plump version and their price is often based on their appearance and color. Currently Madagascar Vanilla Beans are running $200 to $250 per pound which breaks down to $12 50 to $15.60 an ounce. You should get 6 to 8 beans per ounce so the average bean price for Madagascar Vanilla is $1.56 on the lo end and $2.60 on the high end. If you are being charged more than this please do some research on the company and pricing trends

Ugandan Beans (Planifolia Andrews)

Are the same as Madagascar Vanilla beans but grown in Uganda. Surprisingly where the bean is grown, how it's pollinated, harvested, and the curing and drying process all add to the flavor. Ugandan beans seem to have a rather high Vanillin content and the smell of rich chocolate and earthy vanilla tones. Many companies that sell these beans including Amadeus Vanilla Beans suggest "The Ugandan beans are the finest gourmet vanilla beans we are now seeing in the market – surpassing even the finest Madagascar bourbon beans (Amadeus Vanilla Beans. 2021) These beans are worth trying and usually run the same price as Madagascar. Ugandan Beans are running $199.00 per pound to $225.00 per pound and you should get about 160 to 180 beans per pound. The average bean price for these beans is $1.10 to $1.40 per bean.

Mexican Vanilla (Vanilla Planifolia Andrews)

Mexico is often touted as "The Birthplace of Vanilla" and is well known for providing some of the best Vanilla beans you can buy. Most people who believe Bourbon Vanilla is the best you can buy think so mostly because of the name. Although a region makes a difference in reality, cultivation, harvesting and curing is what makes the Vanilla beans amazing.

Most of the beans in Mexico are pollinated by hand though word has it that bee's do lend a hand in pollination. In Mexico you often see their beans cured in wooden boxes that they cover with palm rags. Mexican Vanilla has a smoky tone with scents of Cinnamon, raisin and often cocoa. There is often the same sort of argument you see in sports teams between Vanilla aficionado's on which are better – Madagascar or Mexican. I think they are both outstanding.

Although many people can't tell the difference between Mexican and Madagascar Vanilla, they can definitely tell the difference between the Planifolia Vanilla bean and the Tahitian Vanilla or Tahitensis Moore.

Photo's Courtesy the Madagascar Vanilla Company
https://www.madagascarvanillacompany.com/buymadagascarvanillabeans/#sava

Tahitian Vanilla (Vanilla Tahitensis Moore)

Tahitian Vanilla is unlike anything most people have ever had. Tahitian beans have a milder vanillin flavor that has many flavor layers of spices, cream and caramel. There's an almost floral citrus note that makes it preferred by the best pastry chefs in the world

However, Tahitian vanilla has a higher level of Coumarin that is strictly banned in vanilla extracts in the US due to the possibility of it causing cancer. Sadly it's the Coumarin that adds the rich, unctuous scents to this bean. One might say it's unsafe to buy these Vanilla beans because of the Coumarin content. However, Coumarin is also found naturally in many of the spices and fruits we eat on a daily basis. An example is Cinnamon. Some Cinnamon varieties have as much Coumarin as Vanilla. If you are concerned, do some research.

Tahitian Vanilla beans lend themselves to one of my favorite vanilla recipe's for my "Pirate's Gold Vanilla". To me they remind me of visiting the Islands and there is nothing to compare to these beans.

Photo compliments of The Spice House The Spice House
https://www.thespicehouse.com

Indian Vanilla Beans

These beans are jumping onto the market but it's difficult to find too much information on them. They are advertised as sweet and aromatic. Their flavor tones seem to be creamy and some advertise them as a bit chocolaty.

If a company is saying they source from India please ask them the name of their supplier

Indonesian Vanilla (Vanilla Planifolia)

This is another one I rarely see but hear amazing things about. The Indonesian have a rich smokiness because the beans are often cured over fire. Smoked Vanilla beans are an incredible flavor when made into extracts.

Indonesian beans are often a bit lower on the price scale and would be considered a decent bean. If you can't afford the pricey Madagascar Beans it's not unheard of to buy half Madagascar and half Indonesian beans. The best Indonesian beans I've purchased have come from Amadeus Vanilla. Give them a try next time you want to make Vanilla on a budget.

Chinese Vanilla Beans

It seems China has gotten into the Vanilla Bean market and rumors suggest their beans are not as good as many well established bean producers available today. I was able to find some Chinese Vanilla Beans for sale on reliable website as low as $150 per pound. With the average Vanilla beans floating at the $200 to $225 mark per pound I have to question the low price. That does not mean the beans are bad – that is for the consumer to decide.

A note on
TONKA BEANS

Vanillin, as you know by now, is in many different plants. The Vanilla bean has the highest concentration of Vanillin and the next highest is in TONKA BEANS. Many of the extracts you can buy from Mexico and other countries are made from Tonka Beans and not Vanilla beans. Tonka beans are easier to grow and take less human effort so it's can be better to grow for financial purposes. I'm not going to speak on whether these beans truly are toxic cancer causers but I will suggest you are very cautious when buying your Vanilla Extract to make sure it has not come from these beans. Better safe than sorry!

Buying Vanilla Beans

The Vanilla beans that you buy make a huge difference in your final product. Take this information to help you make the proper choice.

A. Make sure the beans are waxy and darkish. Extract making beans can be reddish brown to dark brown.

B. The beans should be pliable and bendable. Crispy beans may be older but can still make great extract.

C. Grade A , Grade B, Gourmet, and Black/Noir are very loose terms. There's no protocol or oversight so people can use these terms to make themselves extra money. Beware

D. Grade A is supposed to be more plump and have a higher water content. It is suggested these are not best for extracts but after making with both beans I have not been able to see a large difference in flavor.

E. Grade B is supposed to be thinner, more reddish brown, and more flavorful to use in extracts. This is not a guarantee. Some labeled Grade B can really be thin cracked and very poor in quality.

F. Gourmet and Black/Noir Vanilla Beans are yet another money maker "name" that is used to add value to a product a company sells. It's the seller that does this...not the producer. Buyer beware.

F. Cont. I have seen companies selling Vanilla Beans on line labeled as Gourmet for as much as $12.00 per bean and more. This ...is...insane. These beans are only labeled gourmet because they are plump and rich looking and the higher the moisture content, the higher the chances of mold. These simply are not better. Avoid these scams and companies.

G. Always purchase from a reputable source. Companies that use these grading profiles to hike up the price of beans to astronomical heights are preying on your lack of knowledge.

H. Organic Beans is another term used to hike up the price. Most of the farms cant even afford pesticides and GMO is a non existent thing.. To become Organic the farm needs to be certified. Ask which farm they come from to verify. If they wont tell you – don't trust the label.

I. Shorts, Cuts, Splits – Cuts are pieces of Vanilla, that are shorter, older, maybe messier or bent and are not of good enough quality to sell on the market. Shorts are simply beans that did not reach a sellable length. Splits are beans that have split while drying or growing and may still be good but do not have the strong physical characteristics needed to fetch a fair price. Any one of these can be chosen to make into Vanilla powder instead of extract.

J. Be careful when buying Vanilla Powder that it has not come from SPENT BEANS previously used in the extraction process. This powder is often sold as a full flavor powder and it is a scam.

K. TK is also referred to as Grade A and has sometimes been referred to as Gourmet. Verify with farm.

L. Very dry beans happen – They are smaller, brittle, dry, cracked, but can be incredibly flavorful.

M. Seeds – this is another scam area. There are less reputable companies that will take what is called "ground specs" of garbage vanilla. It's easy to take these pieces and pad a product. When buying your seeds or caviar products make sure your seller is reputable.

N. Selling one bean in a container like it's a piece of gods hair is a sign for me to not purchase that bean. That's my choice. I'm not saying those beans aren't great beans deserving of elaborate packaging and insane price. I'm saying I prefer to source from other places. Some companies can use tactics like this to cheat customers and manipulate prices. There are also many reputable companies that use this tactic to sell small amounts. You decide which is which. I am not here to say whose bean is better or if one company is manipulating prices. I just prefer to not buy this way. You do you.... Just remember where they come from.

Photo courtesy of Madagascar Vanilla Company
https:www.madagascarvanillacompany.combuymadagascarvanillabeans/#sava

All that being said – My personal favorite company for purchasing Vanilla beans and asking questions is in Madagascar and will gladly share with you what is legitimate and what is fake. This company is:

Madagascar Vanilla Company. They have excellent prices – as of May 1st 2021 they are $50 to $100 less per pound than a lot of places and the beans make outstanding Vanilla. Frankly – their beans make the best vanilla I have made to date and my customers ask for their beans more than anybody else's. They are also directly related to the SAVA region of growers in Madagascar.

https://www.madagascarvanillacompany.com/#featured-products

Photo's Courtesy the Madagascar Vanilla Company
https://www.madagascarvanillacompany.com/buymadagascarvanillabeans/#sava

A Word on Vanilla Co-Op's

CB

When I first started making Vanilla I joined a co-op because it offered *"Great Deals"* on Vanilla along with ease of purchase, volume discounts, cute Vanilla bean names…I mean this was awesome in my book…Until I started doing my research and realized that "many" of these co-ops are NOT a great deal. Not even a little.

Some of the prices are higher than if you had bought it yourself from the distributor, Some WAAAAAY Higher! I saw a co-op offer Vanilla at $326 a pound! I can get it right now at several places for $250 give or take $10. Some of their co-op prices were the same as the price you could get it at if you spent five minutes looking. So…what's the problem with that?

The problem is you are buying through them at a volume allowing them to get their vanilla for free and make a sizeable amount of your lack of knowledge. Yes – with some of these Vanilla companies you allow "THEM" to buy in massive bulk to get discounts they are not passing on to you. Still don't understand? Let me explain in greater detail.

Let's say Vanilla Co-op A Charges you $250 per pound for Vanilla. Let's say 20 people of the thousands of people they have in their co-op buy a pound at this price. (I'm using the pound price since it's easiest to explain) 20x $250 is $5000. Lets say they can get 10 Kilo's or 22 pounds (a kilo is 2.2 pounds) at a bulk price of $400 per Kilo which is not impossible (in large orders) if you know how to haggle prices. Most companies buying in HUGE bulk orders get an even better discount but lets use this.

10 Kilo's of Vanilla would then be $4000. You paid $5000 for the same Vanilla in your co-op. They got 2 pounds free and made $1000. Now...if this Co-op is attached to any sort of business where they make and sell extract – you are basically helping them get their beans for FREE!

Do your research and see for yourself. If this co-op you have joined is not offering your vanilla around the $200 per pound or $12.50-14 an ounce price range you "may be" getting scammed. (I say may because they may also be paying a ridiculous fortune for their vanilla...but it's unlikely)

Now, there are legitimate Vanilla Bean Co-ops out there that are open about where they get their vanilla, what they pay, and how you are discounted for your purchase. If they are charging more than $15-$16 an ounce they are ripping you off. Find better.

Another thing that bothers me with Co-op's. They tell you to use 1 cup alcohol to 1 ounce of beans. That is more than you need. By telling you to use more – you BUY MORE! FDA guidelines say 13.35oz per gallon is single-fold. Period. Yes you can add more and yes it will be a smidge stronger. Make it however you want is what I say – just be careful how you are getting ripped off.

Lastly, I was on a co-op page today that I noticed was "retailing" their Vanilla beans at $360 a pound. When I asked them why their prices were $100 higher than... ANYONE ON THE PLANET....they kicked me off the page. Realistically I wasn't their friend and I was just using it as a research tool... but I digress... use your intuition and ask questions. If you ask a question and they kick you off their page – they are lying to a lot of people and they don't want them to know.

In the back of the book I have a list of reputable companies that sell Vanilla at fair prices. Their prices also ebb and flow with the market unlike a co-op and their shipping is far faster. Stop making co-op owners rich and buy from one of these companies!

One Positive Note on Co-ops. If they are good at what they do – they do source really good vanilla. Companies will give them the best stuff because they are a large purchaser. If you are only purchasing in small quantities – use them. If you want a pound or more or will be buying regularly – source your own!

The Alcohol

CB

We know the beans we use are the first layer in our Vanilla Extract, the second layer is the Alcohol. Using the proper alcohol for the proper purpose is the key to making extracts that wow the senses and dazzle those that partake in your creations. We all know by the Bourbon vanilla does not contain Bourbon but who says it can't? There is no rule or law that says you have to use Vodka when making your Vanilla.

Anyone can throw a handful of Vanilla pods into a jar and make Vanilla extract. When you take that Vanilla extract to a new level with layers of flavor notes and scents you create a vastly unique and creative product that stands above everything else on the market.

There are a myriad of Alcohol choices to extract your unctuous vanilla. Learning about them and how they can make your finished product amazing is the next step in your journey. One thing to remember is to use 80 proof at the most. We aren't making shine, we're making magic.

A Note on Choosing Alcohols

Artificially Flavored or flavored alcohols should never be used to make Vanilla. Flavored Alcohols are usually made using other extracts or chemical flavors and are not going to turn out a good product. If it says something like Lemon-flavored or Grapefruit-flavored this will be great for a drink but it is not something to use in a Vanilla recipe's.

Infused Alcohols are infused with actual herb's, spices, fruits, beans and more. These, depending on the flavor, are great choices to use as your sole alcohol or in a blend of alcohols you use to make your own special blends. Just be careful your flavors are not overpowering. An example is Cinnamon Infused Vodka. This Vodka makes an exceptional drink but as a stand alone vodka for your Vanilla it is way to strong of a flavor.

Using different alcohols in a blend of flavors and notes is your best choice and in this way you can use small amounts of strongly flavored alcohols in your vanilla making process. Just remember layers, not flavors.

Lets Start with the Basics

The majority of people that chose to make a home made Vanilla chose an unflavored Vodka. The basic recipe is as follows. Buy a Canning jar or Swing Top Bale Bottle/Jar that is about an inch taller than the Vanilla beans you will be using. Your ingredients are usually...

5-10 Vanilla Pods (Random Choice)
Vodka 80 proof (No measured amount)

It's mixed together and stored away. It's usually good after about 8 weeks and if left to age for 6 months to a year the flavor mellows and a depth is created. You can keep this vanilla in the jar, using what you need, and using, discarding, and adding Vanilla pods as you need them. You can partake in that rich bean/seed liquor inside the infused beans. You can add vodka and beans periodically and as Ina Garten did-you can keep this Vanilla percolating in your pantry for decades. This is a perfectly good, simple, Vanilla....but there is no specific recipe and it's...basic. You can do better.

Lets Explore our Alcohol Choices!

As I mentioned above - we start off with the basics.

Basic Clear Vodka: (minimum 80 proof) is your standard choice. It will create a perfectly good "basic" extraction of Vanilla...but it can be a better

<u>Vodka's</u>

The Majority of real aficionado's use a top shelf Vodka to make their Vanilla. The saying goes if you wouldn't drink it, don't use it in your vanilla. In keeping with that we suggest the following 3 Vodka's to make the best Vanilla: Broken Shed, Grey Goose, and Tito's. These are our choices and you are free to use whichever you'd like as there are dozens of other legitimate Vodka's to choose from!

 Grey Goose has a very pure flavor and that is what most people want in their vodka when making any Extract. Grey Goose has been compared to drinking "Boozy Water (Vinepair. 2020)" A Fifth runs about $23 to $29.00

Broken Shed Vodka is an excellent subtle Vodka that subtly adds to the sweetness of your Vanilla. It doesn't have a peppery nose like some vodka's and will pair beautifully with any bean choice. This beauty comes in at $20 to $24 a fifth.

 Smithworks Vodka is a cousin to the ever popular TITO's in that it is triple distilled and charcoal filtered. This is a delicious smooth choice if you want to save a few bucks on the obvious Tito's choice. Smithworks come in cheap at $15 a fifth and is a great inexpensive choice!

RUM

Rum is an excellent partner in your vanilla making and my first choice. The thought of using rum to make my Vanilla excites me. It brings the idea of the Caribbean, Pirates, Island Vacations and the foods of the that stick in our memories. The reason Rum works so well is the sugarcane it's made from adds a level of flavor and sweetness to the vanilla that adds to it's depth.

It's important to know what makes rum great to help you decide which to choose. Rums are categorized by color – darks are barrel aged and have a whiskey flavor, gold's and ambers have had some barrel aging and are the mildest. Rhum industriel are made from Sugarcane byproducts (not as good) and rhum Agricole is made from fresh sugarcane juice. (better choice). Some rums are more sweet than others and sipping rums are going to be best in Vanilla.

You can experiment with different Rums, from dark to light that have all sorts of unique flavor and scent notes that will add a layer of magic to your Vanilla. With the idea to never overpower your vanilla I can think of dozens of rums that would pair well. If cost is an issue for you and you don't want to invest a fortune into making your vanilla I'd stick with the most Basic Bacardi and it will be great! If flavor is your goal consider these choices.

Chairman's Reserve is a fabulous addition as the main alcohol or part of a blend of alcohols you use to make your Vanilla. This delicious sipping rum has a fruity woody flavor and was aged in old bourbon barrels. This screams layers. (Photo courtesy Town and Country Magazine https://www.townandcountrymag.com/leisure/drinks/g9077403/best-sipping-rums/)

If you want the most heavenly finished vanilla product. Mix 50/50 Shipwreck Vanilla Rum with Bacardi Rum and make double fold Vanilla with it and you will have heaven. I still have people asking me "what the heck was that vanilla made with?"…I never tell. Shhh.

Plantation Grande Reserve 5 year Rum is killer in Vanilla! This amazing rum finished in cognac barrels adds sweet honey, creamy caramel and orange peel flavor notes that can easily stand alone as the main Alcohol in your vanilla. (Photo Courtesy of PlantationRum.com https://www.plantationrum.com)

One of my favorite rums for Tahitian Vanilla is made by Parce Rum. Parce 3 year rum has been aged in Bourbon Burrell's so it's absorbed some wonderful bourbon undertones. It comes with it's own heady honeysuckle, caramel and vanilla flavors. This Rum stands alone as the main alcohol for your Vanilla or can dilute a headier spicier rum and become part of a blend. (parcerum.com)

Check out their website at https://www.parcerum.com/english

The next brand of Rum that I often use alone or in blends is Bacardi. Bacardi from light caramel colored rum to the dark rich rum is a go to and a never fail in both taste and layers of scent and sweetness. You can use the majority of them as a stand alone choice or the spicier richer rums easily jump into blends. There is no law when adding or blending alcohols to add to the flavor and scent notes of your vanilla so use these and have some fun.

Take a minute to visit Bacardi's home page for more detailed information.

https://www.bacardi.com/us/en/our-rums/

All of these choices are amazing but my second favorite to add, especially when making Tahitian Vanilla is Captain Morgan. Although all of their rums are superior I stick with 3 and add them to dozens of different Tahitian Vanilla blends.

The Original Spiced Rum is a go to for my favorite "Island Blend Double Fold Aged Tahitian Vanilla" For a solid replacement for basic vodka is the Captain Morgan White Rum. This pairs quite well with Madagascar or Mexican Vanilla pods.

Both of these are great but it's the Captain Morgan Black Spiced Rum that adds some of the best notes to my Tahitian Vanilla. Although too strong and rich to be used as a stand alone Alcohol it's addition to blends is hard to beat. Photo's and information courtesy the Captain Morgan site. Visit for more details.
https://www.captainmorgan.com/en-us/

These are the only 3 options I use from the Captain Moran line. They have plenty of other amazing choices but they aren't great choices/

There are dozens of other Rum Brand choices and you can use whatever alcohol you desire. Always choose a rum that you like the taste of. Read the reviews to help you decide. And above all experiment! Become famous for your specific blend and always consider the flavor notes!

Bourbon

Bourbon is a sexy, sultry alcohol to use when making
Vanilla. The flavor and scent layers in Bourbon pair
beautifully with the unctuous richness of a completed
Vanilla. Madagascar and Mexican Vanilla seem to
blend the easiest with a rich smooth Bourbon the same
way Tahitian Vanilla owned the Rum category.

Most Bourbons have strict rules in how they are made.
All bourbons must be barrel aged with new barrels
and can not contain artificial flavor or color additives.
Bourbon is made from corn, along with rye, wheat, or
malted barley, to add flavor notes and depth. The
barrel aging seems to cut the "bite" of the bourbon and
smooth it out. With any alcohol you choose, if you
don't love the flavor before the vanilla pods, you wont
love the flavor after the vanilla pods.

Liquor.com suggests these are the top bourbons to
drink. These may not be your favorites but if you've
never had bourbon and don't understand it's flavor
profile the place to start is recommendations and
reviews.

One of my go-to's for a blended Vanilla is this little beauty from Widow Jane. The "nose of Nutmeg, cream, vanilla, and a dash of cinnamon and a palate that flirts with maple syrup, almond, cherry and orange (Liquor.com)" will pair extremely well with a Madagascar, Indonesian, Mexican or Peruvian Vanilla. In my opinion it would go with any of them! (photo courtesy internetwine.com)
https://widowjane.com

One of the Bourbons I've often used in my blends is The Devils Cut from Jim Beam. It has intense notes of Vanilla, caramel, and cream, perfect for making Vanilla, along with that heavenly toasted oak flavor. It's a strong heady addition to a blend that you will never forget.
(Photo courtesy liquor.com)

https://www.jimbeam.com/en

Elijah Craig is a well known Bourbon brand and an interesting choice. It's a simple but delicious bourbon that will add a mysterious smoke and warm spice layer to a Vanilla blend. Consider adding a dash of this bourbon to any Vanilla recipe. Your finished Vanilla will be excellent with food or drinks! (photo courtesy Elijah Craig)

https://elijahcraig.com/our-whiskey

Another good suggestion for Bourbons is Woodford Reserve. This bourbon is best used as a layer of flavor and possibly pairs best with Tahitian vanilla due to it's fruit, floral, spice and sweet, woody aromatics. (Photo courtesy Woodford Reserve) https://www.woodfordreserve.com/whiskey/straight-bourbon-whiskey/

Wild Turkey makes a strong Bourbon choice so I will highlight it. Wild Turkey has been a popular addition to drinks world wide and it's well known flavor is an experience. Wild Turkey has several offerings that I would easily add to any Vanilla Blend recipe. The standard *Wild Turkey Bourbon* with notes of Vanilla, pear, and spice and *Wild Turkey Kentucky Spirit* with the rich Vanilla, honey, and almond flavors.

Photo's courtesy WildTurkeyBourbon.com. Please visit their web page and consider purchasing one of these time tested bourbons for your Vanilla blends.
https://wildturkeybourbon.com/about/our-products/

The last highlighted bourbon is Makers Mark and anyone that knows Bourbon knows why Makers Mark is on my list. Even just the basic Maker's Mark Bourbon is a perfect addition to your finished Vanilla. It's lovely oak, vanilla, and caramel notes and the sweet vanilla and caramel flavor is the absolute perfect pairing but the Makers Mark Cask Strength is my favorite. The deep smokiness and strong Vanilla and spice makes this Bourbon a Vanilla makers paradise.

Photo's courtesy MakersMark.com Please Consider visiting their website at
https://www.makersmark.com
To learn more about the flavorful bourbons.

Wild Turkey makes a strong Bourbon choice so I will highlight it. Wild Turkey has been a popular addition to drinks world wide and it's well known flavor is an experience. Wild Turkey has several offerings that I would easily add to any Vanilla Blend recipe. The standard *Wild Turkey Bourbon* with notes of Vanilla, pear, and spice and *Wild Turkey Kentucky Spirit* with the rich Vanilla, honey, and almond flavors.

Photo's courtesy WildTurkeyBourbon.com. Please visit their web page and consider purchasing one of these time tested bourbons for your Vanilla blends.
https://wildturkeybourbon.com/about/our-products/

The last highlighted bourbon is Makers Mark and anyone that knows Bourbon knows why Makers Mark is on my list. Even just the basic Maker's Mark Bourbon is a perfect addition to your finished Vanilla. It's lovely oak, vanilla, and caramel notes and the sweet vanilla and caramel flavor is the absolute perfect pairing but the Makers Mark Cask Strength is my favorite. The deep smokiness and strong Vanilla and spice makes this Bourbon a Vanilla makers paradise.

Photo's courtesy MakersMark.com Please Consider visiting their website at
https://www.makersmark.com
To learn more about the flavorful bourbons.

The Additives

CB

Who says the only thing you can put in your Vanilla is...Vanilla Beans and Alcohol? Nobody! The vanilla you make should mirror what you are using it for. Do you want a special Pumpkin Spice Vanilla for your fall drinks? Do you want a summer Vanilla with hints of Coconut and Lime – why not! This is what you will be baking with and there is not one single thing wrong with creating specific gourmet Vanilla recipes to use in specific gourmet recipe's. Be WILD! Step outside the tiny little Vanilla Extract bubble you have lived and explore the possibilities!

Some of the fun additives I suggest are designed to add layers of flavor or scent to your Vanilla Extract. Be careful that the choices you make do not overpower your final Vanilla. You don't want to add a half dozen cinnamon sticks or you will end up with a finished product that confuses your nose and senses and does not act the way it's designed to. Be creative – but be smart!

Additive's
Oak Barrel Aging Staves!

ℭℬ

Vanilla, that's been oak aged has a flavor profile that is out of this world. You will never find it's equal in a grocery store and even the best specialty stores sell heat induced and sped extractions. When you OAK AGE your vanilla the flavor takes you to a whole new place and I promise you will like it there!

Remember, the goal to amazing Vanilla is in the flavor layers you add. When you use Oak Staves to "Oak Barrel Age" your vanilla in it's bottle you create a product beyond compare. People will ask you how you made it and this tiny little stave will be your secret weapon to flavor!

Oak Barrel aging is generally used to remove the bite from your alcohol and mellow the flavor. This helps your Vanilla by mellowing the bite of the alcohol faster than if you had let it sit and oxidize for a year or more. Oak Staves come in many sizes and char or toast levels. Vanilla is a delicate scent and the darker char/toast staves can easily overpower the vanilla scent. Stick with medium.

Do not just go out and buy oak pieces to add to your Vanilla!! Wood today is often cured and preserved with chemicals and unless you cut down the tree and created the staves – be cautious using them or buy from a manufacture that makes these. Pieces of oak from Home Depot or Lowes are a horrible idea!

What kind Should I get?

We suggest Medium to light char staves and we suggest they are used when making in bulk not small batches. A good rule of thumb is One (1) 3" oak stave per gallon for 3 days to 4 weeks. If you are making a small batch try to safely cut the stave to a smaller size or use for a shorter duration. Once you add this stave you should keep a simple diary of scent and bite changes in your Vanilla. Do not leave in for more than a month. Some people suggest you can but this is not bourbon it's Vanilla and you don't need that kind of aging.

Tips: Tie a string onto the oak stave before adding to your jar so it is easily retrieved.

These companies sell Oak Staves and I have used each of them and find them to be of good quality.

Oak Infusion Spiral
https://www.infusionspiral.com/wine

Amazon.com – just look for oak staves – preferably French Oak Staves

SPICES
This is where adding ...additives...gets fun for me! I have a friend who likes to drink and have parties. Last year (with his money of course) I made him 6 different Vanilla's to use as drink flavorings for his parties. I made Cinnamon Vanilla, Pumpkin Spice Vanilla, Brown Sugar Vanilla, Christmas Vanilla with the slightest hint of peppermint and butter flavor – omg – tasted like butter mints) Root beer Vanilla for his root beer float drinks and my favorite – Orange Vanilla. Yes you heard that right! OMG – it tasted like a dreamsicle! I was super picky with the flavorings and spices I used (yes some of these flavors needed artificial flavoring but they are for specific purposes) and I was careful to use a little at a time till I got the right flavor. On the next page are a couple recipe's – you can always make your own!!

Flavored Vanilla Recipe's with Additives

Christmas Butter-mint Vanilla

✧ Make a 12 ounce batch of Double fold Madagascar Vanilla using 6 ounces Bacardi White and 6 ounces Shipwreck Vanilla Rum. (Use the calculations in back for the amount of beans you will need).

✧ After the Vanilla sits in a warm room for 12 weeks add the French Vanilla Stave – 8 inches of it. Let sit for 6 more weeks.

✧ Next add 8-12 drops Bickford's Butter mint Flavor (you do not want it to overpower the vanilla) Add 3-4 drops at a time – swirl around and smell. Go easy!!! Mint is powerful!!!

✧ Allow to sit another 3-6 weeks and strain. Now – keep in mind those vanilla pods will have a hint of the Butter mint flavor so – dry them out and add to 24 ounces of sugar. Let it sit for a few weeks and you have a magical pairing for the Butter mint Vanilla!!

✧ Now to make this into a fabulous drink additive – get 1 cup of light brown sugar and 1 cup of water – heat over low flame without stirring (or it crystalizes) and turn into a light brown sugar simple syrup. Let it reduce till thick and add to the Butter mint Vanilla. You will go insane – trust me. Again – pair with the Butter mint vanilla sugar and...OMG.

Pumpkin Spice Vanilla

This one is a bit easier.
Take 12 ounces of your finished Vanilla, add ½ to 1 tsp. Pumpkin Spice Powder. Shake and allow to sit a few days to marry the flavors. Shake daily. Restrain when finished. To make this into a drink additive for alcoholic drinks or even coffee if you are feisty make the same simple syrup you made above with light brown sugar and add the finished syrup to the 12 ounces of spiced Vanilla.

Basically – making your own home made recipes for Vanilla and all the amazing uses makes Vanilla far more versatile than you could possibly imagine!

Sugars
Additives

∽

A lot of people add sugar to their Vanilla...and also
Vanilla to their sugar. Sugar and Vanilla seem to go
hand in hand. If you are making the Vanilla as a gift
and you add a tsp. of sugar to both enhance the scent
and flavor that is perfectly fine. Some hardball
Vanilla makers would balk at that but I say do what
makes you happy. When considering adding suger
you must consider which sugar would enhance the
finished product. The best choice? Dark Brown
Sugar. It has a nice burnt sugar flavor that adds
flavor notes to the vanilla that make it the best
addition. If you prefer a you can use light brown
sugar but never use white processed sugar....ever.
Yuk.

Fold's or the strength of the Vanilla

cଓ

Vanilla comes in Single Fold, and Double Fold – The "Fold" is the strength - or is the percentage of Beans to Alcohol. Single fold is the basic FDA guideline required amount of beans to alcohol and double fold is twice the FDA required amount of beans to alcohol.

In some instances you can buy Triple Fold and more but those are for companies such as bakeries and are exceptionally strong. The home baker/maker does not need that and it will only serve to confuse the people you may be making vanilla for. Double fold is my personal choice and the calculation sheets in the back of this book will help you decide how many beans per amount of alcohol to make your single or double fold. The calculations are based on ounces of alcohol to ounces of beans and is very accurate. Despite the accuracy of the calculator in the back of the book – most people still use the simplest 1 Bean to 1 ounce of alcohol ratio for single fold and 2 beans for 2 ounces of alcohol for double fold. This works just fine if you aren't making the vanilla for sale to the public.

Chapter 2
Making Your Vanilla

◆ What are Ratio's
◆ Quick Calculation Charts
◆ Proper Alcohol Dilution Formula
◆ My Basic Vanilla Ingredients
◆ Step by Step Details
◆ Making Vanilla Sugar
◆ Making Vanilla Powder
◆ More Recipe's
◆ Faq's and Hacks
◆ VANILLA BATCH LOG SHEETS©
◆ FDA Guidelines
◆ Cottage Industry Rules and Labeling
◆ Sources

What are Ratio's

A ratio is a unit of measurement or comparison. Ratio's are used to prepare detailed Recipe's where 1 amount is dependent on another amount. For example: say you are making cookies and for every cup of sugar you need 4 cups flour. That is a 1:4 rato of sugar to flour. That ratio needs to be met for each recipe to finish exactly the way it did the time before and the time before that.

When comparing two items to create a ratio it's easiest to use the same unit of measure, such as ounces, ml, or pounds, etc. For a basic Vanilla recipe where someone is using 3 cups of Vodka that would equal 24 ounces. Beans can also be described in ounces so it is the same unit of measurement.

For 24 ounces of alcohol you chose to use 3 ounces of beans. Using math we break this down into their lowest common denominators and get a Bean to Alcohol ratio of 1:8

Most home Vanilla makers do not ever use Ratio's and if you do create a batch log, do not feel like you need to. This is usually for companies.

Quick Calculators

	Bottle Size to Bean	
Alcohol Bottle Size	Ounces of Beans in Single Fold	Ounces of Beans in Double Fold
Mini or Nip (1.7oz)	0.18oz	.36oz
Quarter Pint (3.4oz)	0.35oz	.70oz
Half Pint (6.8oz)	0.71oz	1.42oz
Pint (12.7oz)	1.32oz	2.64oz
Fifth (25.4 oz)	2.64oz	5.28oz
Liter (33.8oz)	3.52oz	7.04oz
Magnum (50.7 oz)	5.27oz	10.55
1.750L (59.2oz)	6.16oz	12.32oz
Half Gallon (1.89L / 64oz)	6.69oz	13.35oz
Gallon (3.79L / 128oz)	13.35oz	26.7oz

Many people ask me, "How many beans should I use per specific bottle size?" The problem with this calculation is the beans displace the alcohol and adding them will overflow the bottle. However, you can use this calculation then macerate in a different container. If nothing else you will know how many beans you need for the alcohol you use. If you want an exact measurement there are calculators online.

Alcohol To Bean Calculator
up to 16 cups or 1 gallon

Cups Alcohol to Bean Ounces (Formula: cups x .8344)

Cups-Alcohol	ML / Liters / Ounces Per Cup	Ounces of Beans - Single Fold	Ounces of Beans 1.5 Fold	Ounces of Beans Double Fold
1 cup	237ml / .237L / 8oz	.8344 oz	1.25 oz	1.67
2 cups	473ml / .473L / 16oz	1.67 oz	2.50 oz	3.34
3 cups	710ml / .710L / 24oz	2.5 oz	3.75 oz	5.00
4 cups	946ml / .946L / 32oz	3.34 oz	5.00 oz	6.68
5 cups	1182ml / 1.182L / 40oz	4.17 oz	6.26oz	8.34
6 cups	1419ml / 1.419L / 48oz	5.00 oz	7.51oz	10.00
7 cups	1656ml / 1.656L / 56oz	5.84 oz	8.76oz	11.68
8 cups	1893ml / 1.893L / 64oz	6.67 oz	10.01oz	13.35
9 cups	2129ml / 2.129L / 72oz	7.51oz	11.26oz	15.02
10 cups	2365ml / 2.365L / 80oz	8.34 oz	12.52oz	16.87
11 cups	2602ml / 2.602L / 88oz	9.18 oz	13.77oz	18.36
12 cups	2839ml / 2.839L / 96oz	10.01 oz	15.02oz	20.02
13 cups	3105ml / 3.105L / 104oz	10.85 oz	16.27oz	21.69
14 cups	3342ml / 3.342L / 112oz	11.68 oz	17.52oz	23.36
15 cups	3578ml / 3.578L / 120oz	12.52 oz	18.78oz	25.04
16 cups	3815ml / 3.815L / 128oz	13.35 oz	20.03oz	26.70

Most Home Vanilla makers use this simple method to determine the ounces of beans needed per cup of alcohol. This per cup method is the simplest way to calculate a great finished product. Calculations above shown using Single Fold – Single and a half – and double.

This is a your basic Quick Calculator for Single Fold Vanilla based on Ounces. (In multiples of 2)

Fluid Ounce to Bean Ounce (Formula: oz x .1043)							
Fluid oz	Bean Ounces	Fluid oz	Bean Ounces for	Fluid oz	Bean Ounces for	Fluid oz	Bean Ounces
2oz	0.21oz	34oz	3.55oz	66oz	6.88oz	98oz	10.22oz
4oz	0.42oz	36oz	3.75oz	68oz	7.09oz	100oz	10.43oz
6oz	0.63oz	38oz	3.96oz	70oz	7.30oz	102oz	10.64oz
8oz	0.8343oz	40oz	4.20oz	72oz	7.51oz	104oz	10.85
10oz	1.043oz	42oz	4.38oz	74oz	7.72oz	106oz	11.27oz
12oz	1.25oz	44oz	4.59oz	76oz	7.93oz	108oz	11.26oz
14oz	1.46oz	46oz	4.8oz	78oz	8.14oz	110oz	11.47oz
16oz	1.67oz	48oz	5.00oz	80oz	8.34oz	112oz	11.68
18oz	1.88oz	50oz	5.22oz	82oz	8.55oz	114oz	11.90oz
20oz	2.09oz	52oz	5.42oz	84oz	8.74oz	116oz	11.48oz
22oz	2.30oz	54oz	5.63oz	86oz	8.97oz	116oz	12.10oz
24oz	2.50oz	56oz	5.85oz	88oz	9.18oz	120oz	12.52
26oz	2.71oz	58oz	6.05oz	90oz	9.46oz	122oz	12.72oz
28oz	2.92oz	60oz	6.26oz	92oz	9.62oz	124oz	12.93oz
30oz	3.13oz	62oz	6.45oz	94oz	9.80oz	126oz	13.14oz
32oz	3.34	64oz	6.67	96oz	10.01oz	128oz	13.35oz

Based on FDA Guidelines of 13.35 oz. of Beans per Gallon. Formula: 1 FL. Oz Alcohol = .1043oz Beans. If you want double fold, double your bean ounces and so on.

Proper Alcohol Dilution Formula

For our next trick we will dilute 95% Alcohol to 50% Alcohol. It's handy to know how to calculate because knowing your alcohol strength is important to proper infusion of Vanillin into the alcohol to make your final product as delicious as possible. To do this appropriately we use this formula

% current a.b.v. Divided by desired alcohol by volume % Multiplied by ml of liquid to reduce, minus ml of liquid to reduce = amount of water needed!

Make sense? Of course not. Let me break it down. First we need to know a couple factors and for Vanilla you need to know the factors BEFORE adding beans. We need:

1. Current Percent of alcohol - let say 95%
2. Desired percent of alcohol - Lets say 45%
3. Amount of liquid you are diluting in ml. Lets say - 1350ml

SO! For todays Explanation we are taking 1350 ml of 95% Everclear and reducing to 45% Everclear. Dandy - lets get started! First remove those pesky % and just use whole numbers. It's easier.

$95 \div 45 = 2.111$
$2.111 \times 1350 = 2850(ml)$
$2850(ml) - 1350(ml) = 1500ml$. So you need 1500ml of water added to your 95% alcohol to get 45% alcohol. Easy peasy lemon squeezie. But...what if I added a whole bunch of alcohols together of different volumes and percentages and I don't know what my starting ABV % is? Well....don't do that again! If you did all is not lost!

You will need to purchase a handy dandy ALCOHOL HYDROMETER. This handy meter and it's tube allows you to determine the alcohol by volume percent of your mixed alcohol content. Get one – you will use it if you are mixing or reducing alcohols. You can pick up a cheap set on Amazon for $15.

So, if you were a naughty little minx and just higldy-pigdly mixed a bunch of alcohols together with random proofs – again this measurement must be done pre beans – then mix your alcohols well in the jar you are using and use the tube and hydrometer to take a sample and measure it. There are video's all over the internet – mostly on brewing sites – that teach you how to use this tool. Trust them – not me. It is rather confusing. Instructables.com has a handy "class" at the following link

https://www.instructables.com/Measuring-Alcohol-Content-With-a-Hydrometer/

If you were smart and decided to do some proper calculating in the beginning and created a "recipe" based on Alcohol percentages Good job! That is definitely the way to go.

My Basic Vanilla Ingredients

⟡

For this batch we're making 4 cups of delicious Madagascar Bourbon Vanilla

- ❧ About 3 ounces of Beans. (2.51 ounces to be exact)
- ❧ 3 Cups Alcohol of choice (try 2 cups of Bacardi White, and 1 cup Shipwreck Vanilla Rum.) Be creative and unique in your choice's if you don't use these but don't let the alcohol flavor overpower the vanilla beans...if you do, you will end up with your own brand of vanilla infused alcohol.
- ❧ 2-4 inches of the Medium Char Oak aging Stave (can use more – start slow and experiment with flavors)
- ❧ Large 32 ounce Jar with Lid. Tall and thin is best to make sure the beans get completely covered.

Step-by-Step Process

☙

- ❧ Slice open each bean pod and carefully scrape out all of the tiny vanilla seeds inside the pod. Add to the jar. Then cut the pod into three 'equalish' sections (or more) and add to jar

- ❧ Top with your Alcohol of Choice making sure to use the proper Bean to Alcohol Ratio's.

- ❧ Shake well and store in a cool dry place.

- ❧ Shake the bean and alcohol mixture as often as you can remember. Daily if you can, couple times a week minimum. I shake several times a day and always get a nice layer of greasy yellow Vanillin after a week floating on top.

- ❧ Label with the date it was made, the amount of alcohol, the alcohol used, the beans used, the ounces of beans total etc. You will want to make this again so you need to remember how. Consider using Batch Logs. These handy dandy sheets take every tidbit of information and coordinates it perfectly.

- ❧ After 8 weeks, if you choose to, add the Oak aging stave. Allow to sit for 3 days to another 4 weeks depending on your desired flavor level. It will mellow the alcohol flavor a bit and add a burnt sugar like flavor that is amazing. It does not make a big difference in recipes like cakes but can in foods like custards and ice cream that rely on the vanilla flavor. It makes them very rich and mysterious. Your friends will want to know where you got this magic blend.

- After removing the oak stave, allow the extract to age another 6 to 8 weeks minimum. This gives you about 16-20ish weeks of aging and that will produce an amazing Vanilla. You can age up to a year but it is not required if the beans are sliced open and chopped. The year long aging process is for un sliced beans as it takes a long time for the alcohol to soak through the outer waxy layer to create the extract.
- Make sure the vanilla pods always stay BELOW THE ALCOHOL for that full maceration period. Make sure the jar is closed tight. The sugars in the vanilla can cause the jar lid to stick so add a layer of plastic wrap between the jar and the lid when closing.
- Make several jars now for the Christmas Holiday!!

Making Vanilla Sugar

❧

Vanilla sugar is an amazing addition to anything from coffee to baking. Anywhere sugar is used, Vanilla Sugar can be used. There are two trains of thought in making this delicious delicacy. 1. Use the beans that have already given their all into vodka to make vanilla. For Vanilla Sugar it's ok as we are just looking for a hint of scent and flavor 2. Use Fresh Beans – Fresh Beans have a very unique smell – not always like Vanilla – but they contain more Vanillin.

I can tell you that, scientifically, once a bean has sat in alcohol for a year it is not only chemically changed, it's likely spent and most of it's Vanillin is gone. So we suggest using 50/50 fresh and used - take a few beans aside when you buy them, cut them open, scrape out the seeds inside, chop them up and stir, seeds, beans and all into your sugar. My basic recipe is:

8-12 Cups Sugar
8 Vanilla Bean Pods (Seeds removed and chopped)
I also spray some of my aged vanilla onto the sugar, allow to dry, then make sure it's not clumped.

Shake daily to break up any clumps and in a few weeks you will have some amazing sugar!! For those of you wincing at adding drops of Vanilla - shhh! just try it.

Honestly - if you have chopped up a bunch of vanilla beans to make vanilla and are read to strain it – DO NOT THROW THOSE PODS AWAY - Definitely dry them out and put them in sugar. Never waste them.

Making Vanilla Sugar

Vanilla sugar is an amazing addition to anything from coffee to baking. Anywhere sugar is used, Vanilla Sugar can be used. There are two trains of thought in making this delicious delicacy. 1. Use the beans that have already given their all into vodka to make vanilla. For Vanilla Sugar it's ok as we are just looking for a hint of scent and flavor 2. Use Fresh Beans – Fresh Beans have a very unique smell – not always like Vanilla – but they contain more Vanillin.

I can tell you that, scientifically, once a bean has sat in alcohol for a year it is not only chemically changed, it's likely spent and most of it's Vanillin is gone. So we suggest using 50/50 fresh and used - take a few beans aside when you buy them, cut them open, scrape out the seeds inside, chop them up and stir, seeds, beans and all into your sugar. My basic recipe is:

8-12 Cups Sugar
8 Vanilla Bean Pods (Seeds removed and chopped)
I also spray some of my aged vanilla onto the sugar, allow to dry, then make sure it's not clumped.

Shake daily to break up any clumps and in a few weeks you will have some amazing sugar!! For those of you wincing at adding drops of Vanilla – shhh! just try it.

Honestly – if you have chopped up a bunch of vanilla beans to make vanilla and are read to strain it – DO NOT THROW THOSE PODS AWAY – Definitely dry them out and put them in sugar. Never waste them.

Classic Madagascar Bourbon Vanilla

☙

This classic Madagascar Bourbon Vanilla is amazing!
- ☙ 13.35oz Madagascar Bourbon Vanilla Beans
- ☙ 1 Gallon Clear Bacardi Rum

This is a bit pricier than store bought Vanilla. Most companies use 200 proof food grade ethanol and dilute it to 40%. Using basic flavorless cheap ethanol/vodka does nothing for the flavor of the vanilla. Do yourself and your baked goods (and maybe friends at Christmas) a favor and use what you would drink. In my opinion Rum and Vanilla are perfect for each other. This basic recipe can be made a million different ways. Just remember at minimum 13.35 ounces of beans per gallon for your finished product to be called Vanilla Extract. (place it all in a jar, seal, shake daily, age for 8 weeks to 1 year)

"Island Girl" Single-Fold Tahitian Vanilla

ॐ

This is a bit more than a Basic Vanilla – it adds Many flavor notes and layers.

- ॐ 13.35 oz. Tahitian Vanilla Beans
- ॐ 77 oz. White Bacardi Rum
- ॐ 31 oz. Captain Morgan's White Rum
- ॐ 10 oz. Captain Morgan's Spiced Rum
- ॐ 10 oz. Shipwreck Vanilla Rum
- ॐ Cardamom Pods (for use during bottling)

Blend all the alcohols and add Vanilla beans. Allow to sit for 6 weeks shaking daily. At 6 weeks open beans and squeeze the rich bean caviar into the Vanilla. Place beans back in jar and seal lid. Age for 6 months minimum. (at 6 months jar the Vanilla adding an equal portion of bean caviar, Vanilla beans, and 1 cardamom pod to each finished jar.) You can add a fresh bean or two to each jar. Allow to age for an additional 6 months minimum before use. Makes 1 gallon.

"Gypsy's Double-Fold Gold" Madagascar Bourbon Vanilla

This Double Fold (or Double Strength) Madagascar Bourbon Vanilla is so insanely delicious I have no words.

- 27 oz. Madagascar Bourbon Vanilla Beans
- 90 oz. Bacardi Gold
- 19 oz. Devil's Cut Jim Beam Bourbon
- 19 oz. Shipwreck Vanilla

Mix all Ingredients together in a 2 gallon glass container (Due to the large amount of beans this will overflow a 1 gallon container). Add Beans and make sure they are covered. Allow to age for 6 weeks. Open and add 4 inches light char oak aging stave. Place in vanilla and age maximum 2 months. Remove stave, and bottle with equal portions of Vanilla beans.

I have a gallon sized jar of this Vanilla that I use as my "mother". A mother is basically your oldest jar of macerating beans. I've added to it over the years by adding spent beans or bits of left over vanilla I made with other alcohols. It's turned into a conglomeration of the best Vanilla's I've ever made and to me it is Gold.

Sourcing Supplies

❧

- ❧ For the Swing Top Bale Jars – I use Specialty Bottle. https://www.specialtybottle.com They have good deals on plenty of other bottles and don't require large minimum purchases but the shipping is high.
- ❧ Another option for bottles is The Cary Company. https://www.thecarycompany.com/16-oz-paragon-glass-jar-63mm-63-405?utm_source=google_shopping&gclid=CjwKCAiA9vOABhBfEiwATCi7GH4TRfAX492k7rH3UtNXf23i-eA2q_CtgYCqTsSnPV0JZPxhD2sHXRoCfGMQAvD_BwE

- ❧ For the Vanilla Beans I will be buying mine from Madagascar Vanilla Company. That is just my preference.
- ❧ https://www.madagascarvanillacompany.com/product/1-4-pound-of-the-worlds-best-beans/

ભ For the Vodka – use any cheap brand. For the
Bourbon I use Jim Beam White Label or Basic
Bacardi. The flavor is proven. You can use a more
expensive Bourbon or a vodka Bourbon blend. Your
choice. About $20 for alcohol depending. For the
Rum I chose Captain Morgan's White, Shipwreck
Vanilla, and will always add a dash of Captain
Morgan's spiced when I can. I've even used a dash
of coconut rum when I use the resulting vanilla for
flavoring spiced cakes and breads.

ભ The oak Aging stick can be purchased on amazon
and directly at their company.
https://www.amazon.com/Oak-Infusion-Spiral-
Barrel-Bottle/dp/B00QSI6SIG

ભ https://north-georgia-still-
company.myshopify.com/products/barrel-aged-in-
a-bottle-oak-infusion-spiral?
variant=31767315054690&gclid=CjwKCAiA9vOABh
BfEiwATCi7GPCjEqpUSJdQMW_YLTkMt2Ufvsb5C
azOThP5fzdKIMn7gm2mhd5t-RoC_4wQAvD_BwE

Whatever alcohol's, beans, or additives you use make
it your own! Be creative but be wise in your choices.
It's expensive to waste Vanilla beans that cost a
fortune on wild recipe's. Be smart!

FAQ's & Hacks

❧

Is _____ alcohol good to use for my Vanilla.
You can use just about anything with a min 35 proof to make your vanilla but note: Beans are expensive! If you choose the wrong alcohol to make your beans and end up with a mess you've wasted your money. It is wise to stay away from Tequila, Gin, "Flavored" alcohol (especially strong flavors) and anything that you would not personally drink. If it's crappy bottom shelf anything that will show in your vanilla.

Can I use 200 Proof Alcohol for my Vanilla and dilute?
Yes! Vanilla manufactures do this to save money on alcohol. They buy 200 proof "ethanol" in bulk and dilute per specifications and standards. You can do this. You will miss out on the flavor notes some alcohol choices can give your vanilla but it will make Vanilla a bit cheaper. Just use the alcohol dilution formula in the beginning of this chapter.

Should I dilute the ethanol before or after I add my beans?
Dilute BEFORE using our dilution formula to 47.5 % alcohol. There is no science to back up using this full strength to extract your Vanilla. People have said that their beans get crispy if the higher proof is used and that could be because the higher proof will extract every bit of life out of your beans – but it can also denature (or destroy/break down the constituents you generally want in your vanilla (Vanillin)

I saw this cool Vodka Jar at the store but It's $60. Is it crazy to buy that Vodka for my Vanilla just because it's got a cool jar?
Heavens yes! If you can use the alcohol in the jar to make your Vanilla then BONUS! I've done it – I guarantee others have. The jar is part of the experience. Just keep in mind – if you are making Vanilla to sell it this is unwise as your final product will cost more than you can sell it for.

Can I speed up the Vanilla Extracting?
Yes! Most people stick whole beans in a jar, cover with alcohol and make this huge production out of it taking a year to make. Lets be for real – the goal is extraction and to do that and do it faster and better – you follow proper extraction methods. Watching a jar sit in a closet for a year is ridiculous and that vanilla will be no better than the vanilla I make in 1/3 of the time. I know this. I compared both and had samples scientifically tested. So how do you speed it up?? A couple ways:

1. If you want to save the beans whole take a large fabric needle and poke a dozen or so holes on both sides of the bean. You want the alcohol to get into the center of the bean to reach the vanillin and this will speed your process up by 6 months.

2. OR...if you are **not saving** the bean pods or will just be using them to make sugar after your vanilla is done – Slice each bean open, scrape out the seeds and cut into small pieces – place all of it into the jar with your alcohol and sit in a warm place (not hot) like a window ledge that gets full sun. (wrap your jar in black fabric or paper – we don't need the sun to see the beans) This will speed up your process by another month or two. Technically you can have perfectly good Vanilla in 4 months that is as good or better than some people who sit and stare at a jug for a year waiting for magic. There is no rule on how the vanilla is made – most of this is just somebody's tradition that made it into the mainstream and became a Vanilla urban legend. Don't torture yourself....BUT!!!!! BE CAREFUL! Alcohol vapors can build up in the jar if it's allowed to get...too warm. Burp your warm jars daily! When "warm" I burp twice a day – caution never hurts. To BURP the jar – remove the lid and air it out. You can also leave the lid just a tad loose.

What if I let my beans sit all chopped up for 4 months and it still smells like alcohol?
So – I've read post after post on Vanilla pages about people complaining they let their Vanilla sit for a year and it still smells like booze so they let it sit another year. I almost spit out my coffee! Here's some hard and fast rules on all ...that.

1. What people don't realize is part of the reason the alcohol flavor mellows after a year is oxidation. It has a bit to do with the beans but let me explain. After any alcohol opens the air hits it. If you are like me and you open and smell your vanilla every few days then you are letting in more air. This air oxidizes your alcohol and that can change the smell and flavor. (if you never open your bottle the oxidation process is super slow.) Like many many years. So shake your bottle daily, open the lid periodically and let the air get it for a second then close it up. This will make a small dent in the boozy smell and flavor.
2. Another reason is dilution. The liquid in the beans will dilute the alcohol (watch your alcohol content).
3. I always suggest using the Oak Stave to mellow the alcohol flavor. I suggest no higher than a medium char and using that for 1 to 2 months will do what sitting for a year does. Again – don't torture yourself!
4. Your alcohol smell is directly related to your alcohol content as well. If you used say...The Kraken Spiced Rum – it has a strong smell due to it's higher proof and contents. All this plays a role. Realistically – cheap alcohol gives an icky cheap smell as well.

Someone told me to use a method called Sous Vide to speed up my Vanilla. Is that safe?
Well....yes and no. A Sous Vide is a low temperature heating method to help the alcohol infuse into the beans faster. The heat opens the pores of the vanilla and swells them a bit and the alcohol moves freely through the bean and this does speed up the extraction process but boy oh boy can it also be DANGEROUS!!! Alcohol boils at 173 degrees. Alcohol vapor begins coming off hot alcohol at I've heard of alcohols exploding in cars and even though this method is usually at around 100 degrees it can still cause a disaster.

Have people been doing this successfully? Yes – many people. Can I do it successfully – sure. But someone can drive a car successfully for 30 years and die in a car accident the next day. I'm just saying be careful of those vapors. You never know which batch is going to cause the problems. If the bottle has a tiny flaw it can open the door for an explosion. Alcohol is flammable. So in this arena I will not tell you to do this. If you choose to, make sure to educate yourself and protect yourself in case of fire. (fire extinguisher for alcohol)

Does the moisture in the Vanilla bean lower the Proof of the original alcohol used? Do I need to compensate for this?
Yes it does and ...honestly – yes and no. Any bean that hasn't been dried completely has a moisture content and anything with a moisture content can dilute your alcohol. However, that dilution is likely minimal. Using a hydrometer and testing mid way through your process is important. If you started at the minimum acceptable alcohol proof (say 70 proof – 35% alcohol) and used some thick plump beans – you diluted your alcohol. You may need to adjust. Just monitor it. Your alcohol content plays many roles from extracting your vanillin to keeping away mold and other ickies. Try to keep your alcohol content above 70 proof. If you don't have a hydrometer and don't want to buy one...just add a shot of 100 proof – you should be fine (should) I'm not in your home to monitor.

If I am mixing alcohols and water do I have to do it a certain way or wait a certain amount of time before adding the beans?
Lord this one made me crack up. I read a post where a man said that if you mix alcohol and water the mixture will heat up and you will need to wait 30 minutes to add the beans. Jesus take the wheel. Yes-adding water to alcohol can create an exothermic reaction – meaning it generates heat. If you are adding water to ethanol or 100% alcohol it will cause it to warm up ever so slightly. But this will NOT harm your beans. I repeat – it will NOT harm your beans!!! The alcohol does not heat up that much.

Does home made Vanilla Smell Good/Sweet/like Store bought Vanilla?

It smells better. A strange thing occurred to me after making Vanilla for some time and smelling my own Vanilla – Store bought Vanilla began to smell like chemicals and nuts. I hear this has happened to many people making a smell comparison impossible. However – do not go by what store bought should smell like. This is made from scratch and will have a sweet vanilla flavor that smells like magic. Store bought Vanilla is processed in vats and sped up by machining. Making your own is no comparison.

Why don't my Vanilla beans smell good coming from the manufacturer? They smell like dirt!

This is not uncommon. Depending on the country of origin (lets say Madagascar) these beans can be cured outside on the ground under the sun and can sit in warehouses for some time and pass through multiple hands before they reach you. Do not despair. If your beans have a bizarre smell – save 4 or 5 aside in a baggie, contact the seller, ask for assistance and let them know you have the beans for a reference. A good seller will stand by their product. HOWEVER it's important to note – The Vanilla beans in their freshly dried state do NOT smell like vanilla. Some have a hint of vanilla...that's it

If I don't use all my beans how do I store them?

I suggest freezing (for short periods of time under a month) them or freeze dying them for longer periods of time. I can't imagine a reason why a vanilla bean needs to sit out of vodka for any length of time. Lol. However – if you are snowed in and can't get to a liquor store and don't have internet to order any you can freeze for a short time or freeze dry for longer periods (don't heat dry it breaks down the good stuff in the bean).

My beans are tattooed. Is that bad?

NO! Those tattoo's are marks the bean manufacturer puts on the infant beans to show who owns them. There is a lot of theft due to the high cost of vanilla beans and tis is a way to deter it. I love the tattoo's. It makes me feel a bit closer to the farm that makes them.

If I scrape the Seeds out of the Vanilla pod does it have any further value?
Yes and it depends on where that bean is in the vanilla making process.
A. If it's a fresh bean and never saw alcohol and you scraped the seeds out for a recipe then put that bean in some alcohol for a week or so and make vanilla. B. If the bean has sat in alcohol for a year and you pulled it out to use in a recipe and scraped out all the inner goodness then this is called a spent bean and yes it still has value for you – not for use in a product you sell... – you can use it to make salt or sugar or dry it out and powder it for your own recipes. It's important to note that you can't use spent beans to flavor anything you plan on selling...

Do I have to add my Beans whole?
No. If you will not be using the beans at a later date to scrape the seeds out of for recipes then no – cut them up. It does speed up the extraction process. If you might use a few then leave a few whole. That's totally fine to mix it up this way.

SPENT Beans. Can I use spent beans to make stuff?
Why yes! As long as it's not something you are making to sell. Vanilla salt, powder, sugar, etc, per FDA guidelines, must be made with fresh vanilla beans. Using spent beans to make these items means the flavor and smell will be diluted. Can you do it for yourself? Absolutely! But if you are caught using poor practices in making and selling spent beans you can be fined by the FDA and shut down. Don't do it. ASLO! Be careful who you buy Vanilla sugar, powder, sat etc from online. If you can't guarantee they haven't used spent beans then buyer beware. It also can't hurt to ask.

Someone told me that CUTTING the beans causes them to heat up and I had to wait before adding to the alcohol.
I'm rolling my eyes. NO STOP it! Seriously! Someone really said this? I understand that some people have to make everything difficult. Some people have to create processes within processes then they tell other people and we get questions like this..

NO! Your beans do not get hot when they are cut and it is perfectly safe to add directly to the alcohol. Does some minute thermal reaction occur when metal is used to slice something – who knows- maybe... likely? But it's minute – the beans likely get more heat from your hand! If it does minutely heat up, it will cool as quickly. No matter what it will not be "unsafe" to add these beans immediately to your alcohol

Can I just grow my own Vanilla at my house or in a greenhouse?
If you have a grow room or live in a tropical climate then YES you can grow your own Vanilla at home. Use some of the seeds from a bean that has not seen alcohol and create a small greenhouse to get them big enough to take outside. There are books on growing Vanilla beans as well as how to dry it out properly to make Vanilla. This is a labor-intensive process and takes experience and knowledge to do successfully...but why not?

Can I use my Vanilla extract to flavor my coffee? But it has Alcohol in it!
You can use your Vanilla Extract for whatever you want!! I mean – if you have to go to work then maybe pouring in a shot of Vanilla is a bad idea but! You can use your vanilla to make the best darn coffee creamer on the planet – that dilutes the alcohol

What is a "Mother Jar"?
Ah the infamous Mother Jar!!! A mother jar, by definition, is a Jar that a very large batch of vanilla was once made in that is used and added to over the years. It's likely got a very strong vanilla flavor and it's kinda vanilla land street cred to say you have a "blank" years old Vanilla Mother Jar. I'm going to be straight with you – I do not like Mother Jars – here's why.

Alcohol, after a period of years, oxidizes, changes flavor, changes proof, can crystalize, and can go bad. This is determined by the seal on the container, how often it's opened, and how it's been diluted (or how many beans have been added).

If you've had that mother jar of Vanilla for 5 years and add alcohol and beans willy-nilly you have almost no idea what the alcohol proof is or what the Vanilla "fold" is, which beans are old, which beans are new and so on. Can you see why I don't like this?? Do the majority of people who have mother jars keep perfectly good mother jars for decades... yep. But I still don't like it. That's me – you do it however you want.

Personally I make at least a half dozen different "designer" or unique flavored Vanilla's and I'm not going to keep a mother jar of each of them sitting around. I sell them too fast to do that anyway. I also want to know that the alcohol proof is above where it should be so bacteria won't grow or mold etc. I want to know the fold of my vanilla when you add alcohol and beans and don't measure anything you have no idea if you vanilla is weak or strong. When you take a bean out to use it in your baking...was that bean an old bean that's ok to use or did you grab a new bean that still needs to infuse in all that alcohol you just added. So – if you chose to make a mother jar – for heavens sake – **keep a "Mother Journal"** and add based on formula's. Keep the new beans in the back or snip the top of the old beans so you know which is which. Etc.

Where am I going to get a **Mother Jar Journal**? Our Vanilla Batch Log book has a Mother jar Journal in the back. It is very helpful and will make that Mother Jar the Queen of the Cabinet!

Blends/Blending Alcohols in your Recipe's

Keep your blends simple and similar to the the flavor of the Vanilla Beans you are adding. Learn the Flavor notes and research the alcohol choices that match.
Remember to use tall thin bottles that are wide enough to hold all the beans. You want the alcohol to cover the beans so mold and fungus do not grow on the exposed parts

Batch Logs

Frankly Batch Logs are important for just about everyone! If you want to remake the exact same Vanilla recipe every single time or if you made Vanilla for the family and they asked for your recipe – you need batch logs.

Batch logs are designed to input your Alcohol information and percentage, your Bean manufacture and percentages of beans, any additives and even the type of bottles you use if you so desire. It can be as detailed or a minimal as you want but whatever you do – use a batch log!

I have created a simple batch log that you can use for your own personal use. You can make copies for you but you do not have permission to sell. If you want to make your own for your own needs – it's not all that difficult. Use Xcel.

My batch logs not only have room to log your ingredients – it can also help you calculate your cost per batch and possibly profit.

Batch #   Batch Name _____

Batch Sequence 1 2 3 4 5 6 7 8 9 10	Fold Strength	(B:A) Ratio ___ oz ___ ml
Born on Date	Strained Date if any	Date Finished
Bean Name #1	Bean Name #2	Bean Name #3
Bean Company	Bean Company	Bean Company
Invoice Number	Invoice Number	Invoice Number
Company Address/Origin	Company Address/Origin	Company Address/Origin
Company Phone #	Company Phone #	Company Phone #
or Purchased From	or Purchased From	or Purchased From
Purchase Date/ Arrival Date	Purchase Date/ Arrival Date	Purchase Date/ Arrival Date
Bean Grade/Length	Bean Grade/Length	Bean Grade/Length
Ounces of Beans	Ounces of Beans	Ounces of Beans
Number of Beans per Ounce	Number of Beans per Ounce	Number of Beans per Ounce
Per Bean Cost	Per Bean Cost	Per Bean Cost
Total Cost This Bean/Recipe	Total Cost This Bean/Recipe	Total Cost This Bean/Recipe
Alcohol #1 Name	Alcohol #2 Name	Alcohol #3 Name
Proof	Proof	Proof
Purchase Price/Size	Purchase Price/Size	Purchase Price/Size
Invl/Company if any	Invl/Company if any	Invl/Company if any
Alcohol cost Per Ounce	Alcohol cost Per Ounce	Alcohol cost Per Ounce
# Ounces Used	# Ounces Used	# Ounces Used
Cost of This Alcohol	Cost of This Alcohol	Cost of This Alcohol
Alcohol #4 Name	Alcohol #5 Name	Alcohol #6 Name
Proof	Proof	Proof
Purchase Price/Size	Purchase Price/Size	Purchase Price/Size
Invl/Company if any	Invl/Company if any	Invl/Company if any
Alcohol cost Per Ounce	Alcohol cost Per Ounce	Alcohol cost Per Ounce
# Ounces Used	# Ounces Used	# Ounces Used
Cost of This Alcohol	Cost of This Alcohol	Cost of This Alcohol
Additive #1	Additive #2	Additive #3
Company Name	Company Name	Company Name
Company Address	Company Address	Company Address
Company Phone	Company Phone	Company Phone
Inv #	Inv #	Inv #
Amt Purchased	Amt Purchased	Amt Purchased
Amount Used	Amount Used	Amount Used
Cost of Additive	Cost of Additive	Cost of Additive
Bottles	Labels	Packaging
Company Name	Company Name	Company Name
Company Address	Company Address	Company Address
Company Phone	Company Phone	Company Phone
Inv #	Inv #	Inv #
Amt Purchased	Amt Purchased	Amt Purchased
Amount Used	Amount Used	Amount Used
Cost of Bottles	Cost of labels per batch	Cost of pkging per batch

Batch #   Batch Name _____

		Batch Rating									
Total Cost of Beans											
Total Ounces of Beans		Bean Rating	1	2	3	4	5	6	7	8	9	10
Total # beans used		Alcohol Rating	1	2	3	4	5	6	7	8	9	10
Average Per Bean Cost		Final Rating	1	2	3	4	5	6	7	8	9	10
Total Cost of Alcohol Used		Customer Rating	1	2	3	4	5	6	7	8	9	10
Total Ounces of Alcohol Used					Batch Preparation Notes							
Average Per oz cost of Alcohol	
Total Cost of Additives Used	
Total Bottle Cost	
Total Label Cost	
Total Packaging Cost	
Misc Fees	
Misc Fees	
Total Mist Fees	
Total Cost of this Batch	
Total Ounces in thes Batch	
Total Cost per Ounce	
Sale Price per Ounce	
Profit per ounce	

Batch Diary by Date

FDA Guidelines on Making Vanilla Products

❧

§ **169.3 Definitions.**

For the purposes of this part:

(a) The term *vanilla beans* means the properly cured and dried fruit pods of *Vanilla planifolia Andrews* and of *Vanilla tahitensis Moore*.

(b) The term *unit weight of vanilla beans* means, in the case of vanilla beans containing not more than 25 per- cent moisture, 13.35 ounces of such beans; and, in the case of vanilla beans containing more than 25 percent moisture, it means the weight of such beans equivalent in content of moisture-free vanilla-bean solids to **13.35 ounces of vanilla beans** containing **25 percent moisture**. (For example, one unit weight of vanilla beans containing 33.25 percent moisture amounts to 15 ounces.) The moisture content of vanilla beans is determined by the method prescribed in "Official Methods of Analysis of the Association of Official Analytical Chemists," 13th Ed. (1980), sections 7.004 and 7.005, which is incorporated by reference, except that the toluene used is blended with 20 percent by volume of benzene and the total distillation time is 4 hours. Copies of the material incorporated by reference may be obtained from the AOAC INTERNATIONAL, 481 North Frederick Ave., suite 500, Gaithersburg, MD 20877, or may be examined at the National Archives and Records Administration (NARA). For information on the avail- ability of this material at NARA, call 202–741–6030, or go to: *http:// www.archives.gov/federalregister/ codeoflfederallregulations/ ibrllocations.html*. To prepare samples for analysis, the pods are chopped into pieces approximately ¼-inch in longest dimension, using care to avoid moisture change.

(c) The term *unit of vanilla constituent* means the total sapid and odorous principles extractable from one unit weight of vanilla beans, as defined in paragraph (b) of this section, by an aqueous alcohol solution in which the content of ethyl alcohol by volume amounts to not less than **35 percent**.

[42 FR 14481, Mar. 15, 1977, as amended at 47 FR 11834, Mar. 19, 1982; 49 FR 10103, Mar. 19, 1984; 54 FR 24896, June 12, 1989; 63 FR 14035, Mar. 24, 1998]

§169.175 Vanilla extract.

(a) Vanilla extract is the solution in aqueous ethyl alcohol of the sapid and odorous principles extractable from vanilla beans. In vanilla extract the content of ethyl alcohol is not less than 35% percent by volume and the content of vanilla constituent, as defined in §169.3(c), is not less than one unit per gallon. The vanilla constituent may be extracted directly from vanilla beans or it may be added in the form of concentrated vanilla extract or concentrated vanilla flavoring or vanilla flavoring concentrated to the semisolid form called vanilla oleo-resin. Vanilla extract may contain one or more of the following optional ingredients:

(1) Glycerin.

(2) Propylene glycol.

(3) Sugar (including invert sugar).

(4) Dextrose.

(5) Corn syrup (including dried corn syrup).

(b)(1) The specified name of the food is "Vanilla extract" or "Extract of vanilla".

(2) When the vanilla extract is made in whole or in part by dilution of vanilla oleoresin, concentrated vanilla extract, or concentrated vanilla flavoring, the label shall bear the statement "Made from ____" or "Made in part from ____", the blank being filled in with the name or names "vanilla oleoresin", "concentrated vanilla extract", or "concentrated vanilla flavoring", as appropriate. If the article contains two or more units of vanilla constituent, the name of the food shall include the designation "l-fold", the blank being filled in with the whole number (disregarding fractions) ex- pressing the number of units of vanilla constituent per gallon of the article.

(3) Wherever the name of the food appears on the label so conspicuously as to be easily seen under customary conditions of purchase, the labeling required by paragraph (b)(2) of this section shall immediately and conspicuously precede or follow such name, without intervening written, printed, or graphic matter.

(c) Label declaration. Each of the ingredients used in the food shall be declared on the label as required by the applicable sections of parts 101 and 130 of this chapter.

[42 FR 14479, Mar. 15, 1977, as amended at 58 FR 2886, Jan. 6, 1993]

§ 169.176 Concentrated vanilla extract.

Concentrated vanilla extract conforms to the definition and standard of identity and is subject to any requirement for label statement of ingredients prescribed for vanilla extract by §169.175, except that it is concentrated to remove part of the solvent, and each gallon contains two or more units of vanilla constituent as defined in §169.3(c). The content of ethyl alcohol is not less than 35 percent by volume.

(b) The specified name of the food is "Concentrated vanilla extract l-fold" or "l-fold concentrated vanilla extract", the blank being filled in with the whole number (disregarding fractions) expressing the number of units of vanilla constituent per gallon of the article. (For example, "Concentrated vanilla extract 2-fold".)

[42 FR 14479, Mar. 15, 1977, as amended at 58 FR 2886, Jan. 6, 1993]

§ 169.177 Vanilla flavoring.

(a) Vanilla flavoring conforms to the definition and standard of identity and is subject to any requirement for label statement of ingredients prescribed for vanilla extract by §169.175, except that its content of ethyl alcohol is less than 35 percent by volume.

(b) The specified name of the food is "Vanilla flavoring".

[42 FR 14479, Mar. 15, 1977, as amended at 58 FR 2886, Jan. 6, 1993]

§169.178 Concentrated vanilla flavoring.
(a) Concentrated vanilla flavoring conforms to the definition and standard of identity and is subject to any requirement for label statement of ingredients prescribed for vanilla flavoring by §169.177, except that it is concentrated to remove part of the sol- vent, and each gallon contains two or more units of vanilla constituent as de- fined in § 169.3(c).
(b) The specified name of the food is "Concentrated vanilla flavoring l- fold" or "l-fold concentrated vanilla flavoring", the blank being filled in with the whole number (disregarding fractions) expressing the number of units of vanilla constituent per gallon of the article. (For example, "Concentrated vanilla flavoring 3-fold".)
[42 FR 14479, Mar. 15, 1977, as amended at 58 FR 2886, Jan. 6, 1993]

§ 169.179 Vanilla powder.
(a) Vanilla powder is a mixture of ground vanilla beans or vanilla oleo- resin or both, with one or more of the following optional blending ingredients:
(1) Sugar.
(2) Dextrose.
(3) Lactose.
(4) Food starch (including food
starch-modified as prescribed in § 172.892 of this chapter).
(5) Dried corn syrup.
(6) Gum acacia.
Vanilla powder may contain one or any mixture of two or more of the anticaking ingredients specified in paragraph (b) of this section, but the total weight of any such ingredient or mixture is not more than 2 percent of the weight of the finished vanilla powder. Vanilla powder contains in each 8 pounds not less than one unit of vanilla constituent, as defined in § 169.3(c).
(b) The anticaking ingredients referred to in paragraph (a) of this section are:
(1) Aluminum calcium silicate. (2) Calcium silicate.
(3) Calcium stearate.(4) Magnesium silicate.(5) Tricalcium phosphate.
(c)(1) The specified name of the food is "Vanilla powder l-fold" or "l-fold vanilla powder", except that if sugar is the optional blending ingredient used, the word "sugar" may replace the word "powder". The blank in the name is filled in with the whole number (dis- regarding fractions) expressing the number of units of vanilla constituent per 8 pounds of the article. However, if the strength of the article is less than 2-fold, the term "l-fold" is omitted from the name.
(2) The label of vanilla powder shall bear the common names of any of the optional ingredients specified in para- graphs (a) and (b) of this section that are used, except that where the alter- native name "Vanilla sugar" is used for designating the food it is not required that sugar be named as an optional ingredient.
(3) Wherever the name of the food appears on the label so conspicuously as to be easily seen under customary conditions of purchase, the labeling required by paragraph (c)(2) of this section shall immediately and conspicuously precede or follow such name, without intervening written, printed, or graphic matter.
(d) *Label declaration.* Each of the ingredients used in the food shall be declared on the label as required by the applicable sections of parts 101 and 130 of this chapter.
[42 FR 14479, Mar. 15, 1977, as amended at 58 FR 2887, Jan. 6, 1993]

§ 169.180 Vanilla-vanillin extract.

(a) Vanilla-vanillin extract conforms to the definition and standard of identity and is subject to any requirement for label statement of ingredients pre- scribed for vanilla extract by §169.175, except that for each unit of vanilla constituent, as defined in § 169.3(c), contained therein, the article also contains not more than 1 ounce of added vanillin.

(b) The specified name of the food is "Vanilla-vanillin extract l-fold" or "l-fold vanilla-vanillin extract", followed immediately by the statement "contains vanillin, an artificial flavor (or flavoring)". The blank in the name is filled in with the whole number (disregarding fractions) expressing the sum of the number of units of vanilla constituent plus the number of ounces of added vanillin per gallon of the article. However, if the strength of the article is less than 2-fold, the term "l-fold" is omitted from the name.

[42 FR 14479, Mar. 15, 1977, as amended at 58 FR 2887, Jan. 6, 1993]

§ 169.181 Vanilla-vanillin flavoring.

(a) Vanilla-vanillin flavoring con- forms to the definition and standard of identity and is subject to any requirement for label statement of ingredients prescribed for vanilla-vanillin extract by §169.180, except that its content of ethyl alcohol is less than 35 percent by volume.

(b) The specified name of the food is "Vanilla-vanillin flavoring l-fold" or "l-fold vanilla-vanillin flavoring", followed immediately by the statement "contains vanillin, an artificial flavor (or flavoring)". The blank in the name is filled in with the whole number (disregarding fractions) expressing the sum of the number of units of vanilla constituent plus the number of ounces of added vanillin per gallon of the article. However, if the strength of the article is less than 2-fold, the term "l-fold" is omitted from the name.

[42 FR 14479, Mar. 15, 1977, as amended at 58 FR 2887, Jan. 6, 1993]

§ 169.182 Vanilla-vanillin powder.

(a) Vanilla-vanillin powder conforms to the definition and standard of identity and is subject to any requirement for label statement of ingredients pre- scribed for vanilla powder by §169.179, except that for each unit of vanilla constituent as defined in §169.3(c) contained therein, the article also contains not more than 1 ounce of added vanillin.

§ 169.182

(b) The specified name of the food is "Vanilla-vanillin powder l-fold" or "l-fold vanilla-vanillin powder", followed immediately by the statement "contains vanillin, an artificial flavor (or flavoring)". If sugar is the optional blending ingredient used, the word "sugar" may replace the word "powder" in the name. The blank in the name is filled in with the whole number (disregarding fractions) expressing the sum of the number of units of vanilla constituent plus the number of ounces of added vanillin per 8 pounds of the article. However, if the strength of the article is less than 2-fold the term "l-fold" is omitted from the name.

[42 FR 14479, Mar. 15, 1977, as amended at 58 FR 2887, Jan. 6, 1993]

This is taken from the actual FDA guidelines available to anyone online. These guidelines are for "Making" the above products and is specific in that you must follow these guidelines if you plan to sell in person or online or advertise etc. If you are making Vanilla for yourself or for gifts you are not bound to these guidelines but they are worth following. Is it missing information...yes it is. Where do you find the missing information – I have no idea. Just do your best.

Citation

FDA.gov. [42 FR 14479, Mar. 15, 1977, as amended at 58 FR 2887, Jan. 6, 1993]. Part 169 Food Dressings and Flavorings. 21 CFR Ch. I (4–1–11 Edition). 169.175 Vanilla extract. 169.176 Concentrated vanilla extract 169.177 Vanilla flavoring. 169.178 Concentrated vanilla flavoring. 169.179 Vanilla powder. 169.180 Vanilla-vanillin extract. 169.181 Vanilla-vanillin flavoring. 169.182 Vanilla-vanillin powder. AUTHORITY: 21 U.S.C. 321, 341, 343, 348, 371, 379e. Page 616-619. Retrieved from https://www.govinfo.gov/content/pkg/CFR-2011-title21-vol2/pdf/CFR-2011-title21-vol2-part169.pdf

Please see the actual publications for more detailed information

Cottage Industry Rules

❧

For years to make or sell any food item you had to have a non-home based licensed kitchen that had to follow very strict guidelines set forth by the FDA, Department of Agriculture, and local governments etc.

A short time back Cottage Food Laws were passed – and each state has different laws and rules – that allowed certain foods that did not require specific "time or temperature controls to determine safety" and in some cases "did not require specific food safety packaging to maintain freshness." Each state has different Cottage Food laws and some states are incredibly strict. These laws tell you which foods fall under that specific state's laws as allowed and prohibited, it lists labeling guidelines for sale, allergy guidelines, where you are allowed to sell an how much you can make each year. It's nice that these things are allowed now but some of the states still have strict policies. You can search this website that has links to many state guidelines that you will need when making Vanilla (or anything else). Just click on your state and it will link you to your state guidelines. There are many sites like this one if this site is not functioning – just search – Cottage Food Laws for _____ and add your state name.

Foodpreneure institute
https://foodpreneurinstitute.com/cottage-food-law/

Labeling Guidelines

CS

The following are good basic Guidelines for Labeling your Vanilla.

1. Name of Product
2. A list of ingredients in decreasing order – highest percentage first, lowest percentage last. You should have a detailed recipe that gives you this information.
3. A net weight by volume listed as per guidelines. Some require it says Net Weight. Some say Fl. Oz, etc. Check your states specific guidelines
4. The name address and zip code of product manufacturer, packager, or distributor. (Basically you)
5. Allergen Information under "Contains": and list each allergen such as nuts etc. see below.
6. Any Actual Nutritional Claims – and these need to be backed up - be careful making any claims in case somebody asks for the science behind it.
7. Nutrition information if your product requires it. Some require product testing as well – know your state.
8. and this statement - "Made in a cottage food operation that is not subject to Florida's food safety regulations."

Example....
MADE IN A COTTAGE FOOD OPERATION THAT IS NOT SUBJECT TO FLORIDA'S FOOD SAFETY REGULATIONS
Chocolate Chip Cookie
Ashley Christopher Bryant 1019 Food Safety Drive Tallahassee, Florida 32399
Ingredients: Enriched our (Wheat flour, niacin, reduced iron, thiamine, mononitrate, riboflavin and folic acid), butter (milk, salt), chocolate chips (sugar, chocolate liquor, cocoa butter, butterfat (milk), Soy lecithin as an emulsifier), walnuts, sugar, eggs, salt, artificial vanilla extract, baking soda.
Contains: wheat, eggs, milk, soy, walnuts
Net Wt. 3 oz.

Thank you for buying this book and trusting me to teach you about Vanilla making. If I have left something out – which is not unlikely – the internet, as you know, has every answer you need. I hope I was thorough!

If you are interested in any of my other books – the Making Chicken Paprikas book is a wonderful detailed step by step book with photos to help you make home made Chicken Paprikas with home made dumplings. It is only 1 recipe but this recipe is rather time consuming and elaborate and deserved it's own book.

I also have a few chapter books that will be coming out on Kindle Vella – Interview with a Fairy Godmother and A Gypsy Witch and Willow.

Having autism I use writing as an outlet and hope you enjoy them! Thank you for letting me into your life and thank you for purchasing this book. Hugs!

OH! And please consider visiting and patronizing some or all of the sources I used in the book. We grow together!

References

ᘓ AmadeusVanillaBeans.com. (n.d.) Home Page. Ugandan Vanilla Beans. Retrieved from https://www.amadeusvanillabeans.com

ᘓ Anderson, Mark C. September 21, 2020. The 12 Best Bourbons to Drink 2021. Liquor.com. Retreived from https://www.liquor.com/best-bourbons-4847374

ᘓ Bacardi.com (n.d.) Our Rums Bacardirum.com. Retrieved from https://www.bacardi.com/us/en/our-rums/

ᘓ Bakingbites.com. August 12 2016. "How to Make barrel Aged vanilla Without the Barrel". Baking Bites. Retrieved from https://bakingbites.com/2016/08/barrel-aged-vanilla-extract-at-home/

ᘓ FDA.gov. [42 FR 14479, Mar. 15, 1977, as amended at 58 FR 2887, Jan. 6, 1993]. Part 169 Food Dressings and Flavorings. 21 CFR Ch. I (4–1–11 Edition). 169.175 Vanilla extract. 169.176 Concentrated vanilla extract 169.177 Vanilla flavoring. 169.178 Concentrated vanilla flavoring. 169.179 Vanilla powder. 169.180 Vanilla-vanillin extract. 169.181 Vanilla-vanillin flavoring. 169.182 Vanilla-vanillin powder. AUTHORITY: 21 U.S.C. 321, 341, 343, 348, 371, 379e. Page 616-619. Retrieved from https://www.govinfo.gov/content/pkg/CFR-2011-title21-vol2/pdf/CFR-2011-title21-vol2-part169.pdf

ᘓ Heddlez, Henrique Gobbi, Abreu, Fellipe. (July 31, 2017) "Why are vanilla Growers in Madagascar Struggling to Survive?". Down to Earth. Retrieved from https://www.downtoearth.org.in/news/agriculture/why-are-vanilla-growers-in-madagascar-struggling-to-survive--58322

ᘓ Hubbard, Lauren. (November 30, 2020) The 18 Best Rums that Make the Case for Sipping. Town and Country. Retrieved from

ᘓ https://www.townandcountrymag.com/leisure/drinks/g9077403/best-sipping-rums/

ᘓ Internetwines.com (n.d.) Widow Jane 10yr Bourbon. Internetwines.com retrieved from https://internetwines.com/products/widow-jane-10yr-bourbon-whiskey?variant=17444612079687&gclid=CwKCAjAsc-ABhA7EiwAjry-j9JpCxtup19A22IAe3rT18srw1HfiSEdirwfxzeM_vKtADlhDqr2x8xoCtWkQAvD_BwE

ᘓ Knkx.org. (August 29, 2014) "A Peace Corp Stint in Madagascar gave Him a Vision of Vanilla". KNKX.com. Retrieved from https://www.knkx.org/post/peace-corps-stint-madagascar-gave-him-vision-vanilla

ᘓ MakersMark.com. (n.d.) Bourbon. MakersMark.com retrieved from https://www.makersmark.com

ᘓ Mochas&Javas.com (September 15th, 2020) "Madagascar, Tahitian, or Mexican Vanilla Types Explained". Mochas & Javas. Retrieved from https://www.mochasandjavas.com/vanilla-types-explained/

ᘓ NaturesNurture.com. (n.d.) Indian Vanilla Beans. Tharakan and Company. Retrieved from http://www.tharakanandcompany.com/VanillaInIndia.htm

ᘓ Parcerum.com (n.d.) Our Rums. Parcerum.com retrieved from https://www.parcerum.com/english

Plantation Rum Company. "Our Rums" Retrieved from
https://www.plantationrum.com
Sandoval, M.(September 30, 2011). Vanilla Lesson Plan.
FamilyConsumerScience.com. Retrieved from
https://www.familyconsumersciences.com/2011/09/vanilla-lesson-plan/
Slofoodgroup. (n.d.) Gourmet Madagascar Vanilla Beans Planifolia. SloFoodGroup.
Retreived from
https://www.slofoodgroup.com/products/gourmet-madagascar-vanilla
Specialtybottle.com. (n.d.). Swing Top Bottles. SpecialtyBottle.com. Retrieved from
Spicesinc.com (n.d.) Spice Cabinet 101: Vanilla. Spicesinc.com. Retrieved from
https://www.specialtybottle.com/glass-bottles/swing-top
https://www.spicesinc.com/p-5409-spice-cabinet-101-vanilla.aspx
Thespicehouse.com. (January 8th, 2020) A taste of Paradise:
Tahitian Vanilla Bean. Retrieved from
https://www.thespicehouse.com/blogs/news/a-taste-of-paradise-tahitian-vanilla-
beans
Town and Country Magazine. 18 Best Rums That make The Case For Sipping.
Retrieved from
https://www.townandcountrymag.com/leisure/drinks/g9077403/best-sipping-
rums/
Vanillapura.com (n.d.) How are Vanilla Beans Harvested. Vanillapura.com.
Retrieved from
Vinepair.com. (n.d.) "The 20 Best Vodka Brands of 2020" retrieved from
https://vinepair.com/buy-this-booze/20-best-vodka-brands-2020/
https://www.vanillapura.com/pages/how-are-vanilla-beans-harvested
WildTurkeyBourbon.com. (n.d.) Our Products.. WildTurkeyBourbon.com Retrieved
from https://wildturkeybourbon.com/about/our-products/
WoodfordReserve.com (n.d.) The Worlds Finest Bourbon. WoodfordReserve.com.
Retrieved from
https://www.woodfordreserve.com/?gclid=CjwKCAiAgc-ABhA7EiwAjev-
j0hpvfZSTZYavmNEXs7V3Q7ax94Tx6-C-
bQSYxdysaAp4psvceoU2BoCHzUQAvD_BwE

Extra Batch Logs and Recipe Sheets

℘

I've added a few extra pages for you to make your life convenient so you can use this book as not just a directional guide to making vanilla but your own personal recipe book with batch logs. I hope they come in handy for you!!

Simple Vanilla Recipe

Born on Date _____ Strain Date _____

Bottle Date _____ Finished ounces : _____

Recipe Name _____

Alcohol #1 _____ Oz. _____

Alcohol #2 _____ Oz. _____

Alcohol #3 _____ Oz. _____

Alcohol #4 _____ Oz. _____

Alcohol #5 _____ Oz. _____

Bean Brand _____

Ounces used _____

Additives #1 _____Date added _____

Additives #2 _____Date added _____

Notes _____

_____

_____

Batch #

Batch Name _____

Batch Sequence	1 2 3 4 5 6 7 8 9 10		
Born on Date		Fold Strength	(B-A) Ratio oz ml
Bean Name #1		Strained Date if any	Date Finished
Bean Company		Bean Name #2	Bean Name #3
Invoice Number		Bean Company	Bean Company
Company Address/Origin		Invoice Number	Invoice Number
Company Phone #		Company Address/Origin	Company Address/Origin
or Purchased From		Company Phone #	Company Phone #
Purchase Date/ Arrival Date		or Purchased From	or Purchased From
Bean Grade/Length		Purchase Date/ Arrival Date	Purchase Date/ Arrival Date
Ounces of Beans		Bean Grade/Length	Bean Grade/Length
Number of Beans per Ounce		Ounces of Beans	Ounces of Beans
Per Bean Cost		Number of Beans per Ounce	Number of Beans per Ounce
Total Cost This Bean/Recipe		Per Bean Cost	Per Bean Cost
Alcohol #1 Name		Total Cost This Bean/Recipe	Total Cost This Bean/Recipe
Proof		Alcohol #2 Name	Alcohol #3 Name
Purchase Price/Size		Proof	Proof
Invit/Company if any		Purchase Price/Size	Purchase Price/Size
Alcohol cost Per Ounce		Invit/Company if any	Invit/Company if any
# Ounces Used		Alcohol cost Per Ounce	Alcohol cost Per Ounce
Cost of This Alcohol		# Ounces Used	# Ounces Used
Alcohol #4 Name		Cost of This Alcohol	Cost of This Alcohol
Proof		Alcohol #5 Name	Alcohol #6 Name
Purchase Price/Size		Proof	Proof
Invit/Company if any		Purchase Price/Size	Purchase Price/Size
Alcohol cost Per Ounce		Invit/Company if any	Invit/Company if any
# Ounces Used		Alcohol cost Per Ounce	Alcohol cost Per Ounce
Cost of This Alcohol		# Ounces Used	# Ounces Used
Additive #1		Cost of This Alcohol	Cost of This Alcohol
Company Name		Additive #2	Additive #3
Company Address		Company Name	Company Name
Company Phone		Company Address	Company Address
Inv #		Company Phone	Company Phone
Amt Purchased		Inv #	Inv #
Amount Used		Amt Purchased	Amt Purchased
Cost of Additive		Amount Used	Amoount Used
Bottles		Cost of Additive	Cost of Additive
Company Name		Labels	Packaging
Company Address		Company Name	Company Name
Company Phone		Company Address	Company Address
Inv #		Company Phone	Company Phone
Amt Purchased		Inv #	Inv #
Amount Used		Amt Purchased	Amt Purchased
Cost of Bottles		Amount Used	Amount Used
		Cost of labels per batch	Cost of pkging per batch

Batch

Batch Name

Total Cost of Beans	
Total Ounces of Beans	
Total # beans used	
Average Per Bean Cost	
Total Cost of Alcohol Used	
Total Ounces of Alcohol Used	
Average Per oz cost of Alcohol	
Total Cost of Additives Used	
Total Bottle Cost	
Total Label Cost	
Total Packaging Cost	
Misc Fees	
Misc Fees	
Total Mist Fees	
Total Cost of this Batch	
Total Ounces in thes Batch	
Total Cost per Ounce	
Sale Price per Ounce	
Profit per ounce	

Batch Rating

	1	2	3	4	5	6	7	8	9	10
Bean Rating	1	2	3	4	5	6	7	8	9	10
Alcohol Rating	1	2	3	4	5	6	7	8	9	10
Final Rating	1	2	3	4	5	6	7	8	9	10
Customer Rating	1	2	3	4	5	6	7	8	9	10

Batch Preparation Notes

Batch Diary by Date

Simple Vanilla Recipe

Born on Date _____ Strain Date _____

Bottle Date _____ Finished ounces _____

Recipe Name _____

Alcohol #1 _____ Oz. _____

Alcohol #2 _____ Oz. _____

Alcohol #3 _____ Oz. _____

Alcohol #4 _____ Oz. _____

Alcohol #5 _____ Oz. _____

Bean Brand _____

Ounces used _____

Additives #1 _____Date added _____

Additives #2 _____Date added _____

Notes _____

_____

_____

Batch #   Batch Name

	1 2 3 4 5 6 7 8 9 10		
Batch Sequence		Fold Strength	(B-A) Ratio oz ml
Born on Date		Strained Date if any	Date Finished
Bean Name #1		Bean Name #2	Bean Name #3
Bean Company		Bean Company	Bean Company
Invoice Number		Invoice Number	Invoice Number
Company Address/Origin		Company Address/Origin	Company Address/Origin
Company Phone #		Company Phone #	Company Phone #
or Purchased From		or Purchased From	or Purchased From
Purchase Date/ Arrival Date		Purchase Date/ Arrival Date	Purchase Date/ Arrival Date
Bean Grade/Length		Bean Grade/Length	Bean Grade/Length
Ounces of Beans		Ounces of Beans	Ounces of Beans
Number of Beans per Ounce		Number of Beans per Ounce	Number of Beans per Ounce
Per Bean Cost		Per Bean Cost	Per Bean Cost
Total Cost This Bean/Recipe		Total Cost This Bean/Recipe	Total Cost This Bean/Recipe
Alcohol #1 Name		Alcohol #2 Name	Alcohol #3 Name
Proof		Proof	Proof
Purchase Price/Size		Purchase Price/Size	Purchase Price/Size
Invit/Company if any		Invit/Company if any	Invit/Company if any
Alcohol cost Per Ounce		Alcohol cost Per Ounce	Alcohol cost Per Ounce
# Ounces Used		# Ounces Used	# Ounces Used
Cost of This Alcohol		Cost of This Alcohol	Cost of This Alcohol
Alcohol #4 Name		Alcohol #5 Name	Alcohol #6 Name
Proof		Proof	Proof
Purchase Price/Size		Purchase Price/Size	Purchase Price/Size
Invit/Company if any		Invit/Company if any	Invit/Company if any
Alcohol cost Per Ounce		Alcohol cost Per Ounce	Alcohol cost Per Ounce
# Ounces Used		# Ounces Used	# Ounces Used
Cost of This Alcohol		Cost of This Alcohol	Cost of This Alcohol
Additive #1		Additive #2	Additive #3
Company Name		Company Name	Company Name
Company Address		Company Address	Company Address
Company Phone		Company Phone	Company Phone
Inv #		Inv #	Inv #
Amt Purchased		Amt Purchased	Amt Purchased
Amount Used		Amount Used	Amoount Used
Cost of Additive		Cost of Additive	Cost of Additive
Bottles		Labels	Packaging
Company Name		Company Name	Company Name
Company Address		Company Address	Company Address
Company Phone		Company Phone	Company Phone
Inv #		Inv #	Inv #
Amt Purchased		Amt Purchased	Amt Purchased
Amount Used		Amount Used	Amount Used
Cost of Bottles		Cost of labels per batch	Cost of pkging per batch

Batch #_____   Batch Name _____

Total Cost of Beans	
Total Ounces of Beans	
Total # beans used	
Average Per Bean Cost	
Total Cost of Alcohol Used	
Total Ounces of Alcohol Used	
Average Per oz cost of Alcohol	
Total Cost of Additiwes Used	
Total Bottle Cost	
Total Label Cost	
Total Packaging Cost	
Misc Fees	
Misc Fees	
Total Mist Fees	
Total Cost of this Batch	
Total Ounces in thes Batch	
Total Cost per Ounce	
Sale Price per Ounce	
Profit per ounce	

Batch Rating

Bean Rating	1	2	3	4	5	6	7	8	9	10
Alcohol Rating	1	2	3	4	5	6	7	8	9	10
Final Rating	1	2	3	4	5	6	7	8	9	10
Customer Rating	1	2	3	4	5	6	7	8	9	10

Batch Preparation Notes

Batch Diary by Date

Simple Vanilla Recipe

Born on Date _____ Strain Date _____

Bottle Date _____ Finished ounces _____

Recipe Name _____

Alcohol #1 _____ Oz. _____

Alcohol #2 _____ Oz. _____

Alcohol #3 _____ Oz. _____

Alcohol #4 _____ Oz. _____

Alcohol #5 _____ Oz. _____

Bean Brand _____

Ounces used _____

Additives #1 _____Date added _____

Additives #2 _____Date added _____

Notes _____

_____

_____

Batch #   Batch Name _____

Batch Sequence: 1 2 3 4 5 6 7 8 9 10

Column 1	Column 2	Column 3
Born on Date	Fold Strength	(B-A) Ratio oz ml
	Strained Date if any	Date Finished
Bean Name #1	Bean Name #2	Bean Name #3
Bean Company	Bean Company	Bean Company
Invoice Number	Invoice Number	Invoice Number
Company Address/Origin	Company Address/Origin	Company Address/Origin
Company Phone # or Purchased From	Company Phone # or Purchased From	Company Phone # or Purchased From
Purchase Date/ Arrival Date	Purchase Date/ Arrival Date	Purchase Date/ Arrival Date
Bean Grade/Length	Bean Grade/Length	Bean Grade/Length
Ounces of Beans	Ounces of Beans	Ounces of Beans
Number of Beans per Ounce	Number of Beans per Ounce	Number of Beans per Ounce
Per Bean Cost	Per Bean Cost	Per Bean Cost
Total Cost This Bean/Recipe	Total Cost This Bean/Recipe	Total Cost This Bean/Recipe
Alcohol #1 Name	Alcohol #2 Name	Alcohol #3 Name
Proof	Proof	Proof
Purchase Price/Size	Purchase Price/Size	Purchase Price/Size
Invl/Company if any	Invl/Company if any	Invl/Company if any
Alcohol cost Per Ounce	Alcohol cost Per Ounce	Alcohol cost Per Ounce
# Ounces Used	# Ounces Used	# Ounces Used
Cost of This Alcohol	Cost of This Alcohol	Cost of This Alcohol
Alcohol #4 Name	Alcohol #5 Name	Alcohol #6 Name
Proof	Proof	Proof
Purchase Price/Size	Purchase Price/Size	Purchase Price/Size
Invl/Company if any	Invl/Company if any	Invl/Company if any
Alcohol cost Per Ounce	Alcohol cost Per Ounce	Alcohol cost Per Ounce
# Ounces Used	# Ounces Used	# Ounces Used
Cost of This Alcohol	Cost of This Alcohol	Cost of This Alcohol
Additive #1	Additive #2	Additive #3
Company Name	Company Name	Company Name
Company Address	Company Address	Company Address
Company Phone	Company Phone	Company Phone
Inv #	Inv #	Inv #
Amt Purchased	Amt Purchased	Amt Purchased
Amount Used	Amount Used	Amount Used
Cost of Additive	Cost of Additive	Cost of Additive
Bottles	Labels	Packaging
Company Name	Company Name	Company Name
Company Address	Company Address	Company Address
Company Phone	Company Phone	Company Phone
Inv #	Inv #	Inv #
Amt Purchased	Amt Purchased	Amt Purchased
Amount Used	Amount Used	Amount Used
Cost of Bottles	Cost of labels per batch	Cost of pkging per batch

Batch # _____   Batch Name _____

Total Cost of Beans	
Total Ounces of Beans	
Total # beans used	
Average Per Bean Cost	
Total Cost of Alcohol Used	
Total Ounces of Alcohol Used	
Average Per oz cost of Alcohol	
Total Cost of Additives Used	
Total Bottle Cost	
Total Label Cost	
Total Packaging Cost	
Misc Fees	
Misc Fees	
Total Misc Fees	
Total Cost of this Batch	
Total Ounces in thes Batch	
Total Cost per Ounce	
Sale Price per Ounce	
Profit per ounce	

Batch Rating

	1	2	3	4	5	6	7	8	9	10
Bean Rating	1	2	3	4	5	6	7	8	9	10
Alcohol Rating	1	2	3	4	5	6	7	8	9	10
Final Rating	1	2	3	4	5	6	7	8	9	10
Customer Rating	1	2	3	4	5	6	7	8	9	10

Batch Preparation Notes

Batch Diary by Date

Simple Vanilla Recipe

Born on Date _____ Strain Date _____

Bottle Date _____ Finished ounces _____

Recipe Name _____

Alcohol #1 _____ Oz. _____

Alcohol #2 _____ Oz. _____

Alcohol #3 _____ Oz. _____

Alcohol #4 _____ Oz. _____

Alcohol #5 _____ Oz. _____

Bean Brand _____

Ounces used _____

Additives #1 _____Date added _____

Additives #2 _____Date added _____

Notes _____

_____

_____

Batch

Batch Name

Column 1	Column 2	Column 3
Batch Sequence 1 2 3 4 5 6 7 8 9 10	Fold Strength	(B-A) Ratio oz ml
Born on Date	Strained Date if any	Date Finished
Bean Name #1	Bean Name #2	Bean Name #3
Bean Company	Bean Company	Bean Company
Invoice Number	Invoice Number	Invoice Number
Company Address/Origin	Company Address/Origin	Company Address/Origin
Company Phone #	Company Phone #	Company Phone #
or Purchased From	or Purchased From	or Purchased From
Purchase Date/ Arrival Date	Purchase Date/ Arrival Date	Purchase Date/ Arrival Date
Bean Grade/Length	Bean Grade/Length	Bean Grade/Length
Ounces of Beans	Ounces of Beans	Ounces of Beans
Number of Beans per Ounce	Number of Beans per Ounce	Number of Beans per Ounce
Per Bean Cost	Per Bean Cost	Per Bean Cost
Total Cost This Bean/Recipe	Total Cost This Bean/Recipe	Total Cost This Bean/Recipe
Alcohol #1 Name	Alcohol #2 Name	Alcohol #3 Name
Proof	Proof	Proof
Purchase Price/Size	Purchase Price/Size	Purchase Price/Size
Invl/Company if any	Invl/Company if any	Invl/Company if any
Alcohol cost Per Ounce	Alcohol cost Per Ounce	Alcohol cost Per Ounce
# Ounces Used	# Ounces Used	# Ounces Used
Cost of This Alcohol	Cost of This Alcohol	Cost of This Alcohol
Alcohol #4 Name	Alcohol #5 Name	Alcohol #6 Name
Proof	Proof	Proof
Purchase Price/Size	Purchase Price/Size	Purchase Price/Size
Invl/Company if any	Invl/Company if any	Invl/Company if any
Alcohol cost Per Ounce	Alcohol cost Per Ounce	Alcohol cost Per Ounce
# Ounces Used	# Ounces Used	# Ounces Used
Cost of This Alcohol	Cost of This Alcohol	Cost of This Alcohol
Additive #1	Additive #2	Additive #3
Company Name	Company Name	Company Name
Company Address	Company Address	Company Address
Company Phone	Company Phone	Company Phone
Inv #	Inv #	Inv #
Amt Purchased	Amt Purchased	Amt Purchased
Amount Used	Amount Used	Amount Used
Cost of Additive	Cost of Additive	Cost of Additive
Bottles	Labels	Packaging
Company Name	Company Name	Company Name
Company Address	Company Address	Company Address
Company Phone	Company Phone	Company Phone
Inv #	Inv #	Inv #
Amt Purchased	Amt Purchased	Amt Purchased
Amount Used	Amount Used	Amount Used
Cost of Bottles	Cost of labels per batch	Cost of pkging per batch

Batch

Batch Name

Total Cost of Beans	
Total Ounces of Beans	
Total # beans used	
Average Per Bean Cost	
Total Cost of Alcohol Used	
Total Ounces of Alcohol Used	
Average Per oz cost of Alcohol	
Total Cost of Additives Used	
Total Bottle Cost	
Total Label Cost	
Total Packaging Cost	
Misc Fees	
Misc Fees	
Total Mist Fees	
Total Cost of this Batch	
Total Ounces in thes Batch	
Total Cost per Ounce	
Sale Price per Ounce	
Profit per ounce	

Batch Rating

	1	2	3	4	5	6	7	8	9	10
Bean Rating	1	2	3	4	5	6	7	8	9	10
Alcohol Rating	1	2	3	4	5	6	7	8	9	10
Final Rating	1	2	3	4	5	6	7	8	9	10
Customer Rating	1	2	3	4	5	6	7	8	9	10

Batch Preparation Notes

Batch Diary by Date

Simple Vanilla Recipe

Born on Date _____ Strain Date _____

Bottle Date _____ Finished ounces _____

Recipe Name _____

Alcohol #1 _____ Oz. _____

Alcohol #2 _____ Oz. _____

Alcohol #3 _____ Oz. _____

Alcohol #4 _____ Oz. _____

Alcohol #5 _____ Oz. _____

Bean Brand _____

Ounces used _____

Additives #1 _____Date added _____

Additives #2 _____Date added _____

Notes _____

_____

_____

Batch #   Batch Name _____

Batch Sequence: 1 2 3 4 5 6 7 8 9 10

Column 1	Column 2	Column 3
Born on Date	Strained Date if any	(B-A) Ratio oz ml
		Date Finished
Bean Name #1	Bean Name #2	Bean Name #3
Bean Company	Bean Company	Bean Company
Invoice Number	Invoice Number	Invoice Number
Company Address/Origin	Company Address/Origin	Company Address/Origin
Company Phone #	Company Phone #	Company Phone #
or Purchased From	or Purchased From	or Purchased From
Purchase Date/ Arrival Date	Purchase Date/ Arrival Date	Purchase Date/ Arrival Date
Bean Grade/Length	Bean Grade/Length	Bean Grade/Length
Ounces of Beans	Ounces of Beans	Ounces of Beans
Number of Beans per Ounce	Number of Beans per Ounce	Number of Beans per Ounce
Per Bean Cost	Per Bean Cost	Per Bean Cost
Total Cost This Bean/Recipe	Total Cost This Bean/Recipe	Total Cost This Bean/Recipe
Alcohol #1 Name	Alcohol #2 Name	Alcohol #3 Name
Proof	Proof	Proof
Purchase Price/Size	Purchase Price/Size	Purchase Price/Size
Invit/Company if any	Invit/Company if any	Invit/Company if any
Alcohol cost Per Ounce	Alcohol cost Per Ounce	Alcohol cost Per Ounce
# Ounces Used	# Ounces Used	# Ounces Used
Cost of This Alcohol	Cost of This Alcohol	Cost of This Alcohol
Alcohol #4 Name	Alcohol #5 Name	Alcohol #6 Name
Proof	Proof	Proof
Purchase Price/Size	Purchase Price/Size	Purchase Price/Size
Invit/Company if any	Invit/Company if any	Invit/Company if any
Alcohol cost Per Ounce	Alcohol cost Per Ounce	Alcohol cost Per Ounce
# Ounces Used	# Ounces Used	# Ounces Used
Cost of This Alcohol	Cost of This Alcohol	Cost of This Alcohol
Additive #1	Additive #2	Additive #3
Company Name	Company Name	Company Name
Company Address	Company Address	Company Address
Company Phone	Company Phone	Company Phone
Inv #	Inv #	Inv #
Amt Purchased	Amt Purchased	Amt Purchased
Amount Used	Amount Used	Amount Used
Cost of Additive	Cost of Additive	Cost of Additive
Bottles	Labels	Packaging
Company Name	Company Name	Company Name
Company Address	Company Address	Company Address
Company Phone	Company Phone	Company Phone
Inv #	Inv #	Inv #
Amt Purchased	Amt Purchased	Amt Purchased
Amount Used	Amount Used	Amount Used
Cost of Bottles	Cost of labels per batch	Cost of pkging per batch

Batch

Batch Name

Total Cost of Beans	
Total Ounces of Beans	
Total # beans used	
Average Per Bean Cost	
Total Cost of Alcohol Used	
Total Ounces of Alcohol Used	
Average Per oz cost of Alcohol	
Total Cost of Addititives Used	
Total Bottle Cost	
Total Label Cost	
Total Packaging Cost	
Misc Fees	
Misc Fees	
Total Misc Fees	
Total Cost of this Batch	
Total Ounces in thes Batch	
Total Cost per Ounce	
Sale Price per Ounce	
Profit per ounce	

Batch Rating

Bean Rating	1	2	3	4	5	6	7	8	9	10
Alcohol Rating	1	2	3	4	5	6	7	8	9	10
Final Rating	1	2	3	4	5	6	7	8	9	10
Customer Rating	1	2	3	4	5	6	7	8	9	10

Batch Preparation Notes

Batch Diary by Date

Simple Vanilla Recipe

Born on Date _____ Strain Date _____

Bottle Date _____ Finished ounces _____

Recipe Name _____

Alcohol #1 _____ Oz. _____

Alcohol #2 _____ Oz. _____

Alcohol #3 _____ Oz. _____

Alcohol #4 _____ Oz. _____

Alcohol #5 _____ Oz. _____

Bean Brand _____

Ounces used _____

Additives #1 _____Date added _____

Additives #2 _____Date added _____

Notes _____

_____

_____

Batch

Batch Name

Batch Sequence 1 2 3 4 5 6 7 8 9 10	Fold Strength	(B-A) Ratio oz ml
Born on Date	Strained Date if any	Date Finished
Bean Name #1	Bean Name #2	Bean Name #3
Bean Company	Bean Company	Bean Company
Invoice Number	Invoice Number	Invoice Number
Company Address/Origin	Company Address/Origin	Company Address/Origin
Company Phone #	Company Phone #	Company Phone #
or Purchased From	or Purchased From	or Purchased From
Purchase Date/ Arrival Date	Purchase Date/ Arrival Date	Purchase Date/ Arrival Date
Bean Grade/Length	Bean Grade/Length	Bean Grade/Length
Ounces of Beans	Ounces of Beans	Ounces of Beans
Number of Beans per Ounce	Number of Beans per Ounce	Number of Beans per Ounce
Per Bean Cost	Per Bean Cost	Per Bean Cost
Total Cost This Bean/Recipe	Total Cost This Bean/Recipe	Total Cost This Bean/Recipe
Alcohol #1 Name	Alcohol #2 Name	Alcohol #3 Name
Proof	Proof	Proof
Purchase Price/Size	Purchase Price/Size	Purchase Price/Size
Invl/Company if any	Invl/Company if any	Invl/Company if any
Alcohol cost Per Ounce	Alcohol cost Per Ounce	Alcohol cost Per Ounce
# Ounces Used	# Ounces Used	# Ounces Used
Cost of This Alcohol	Cost of This Alcohol	Cost of This Alcohol
Alcohol #4 Name	Alcohol #5 Name	Alcohol #6 Name
Proof	Proof	Proof
Purchase Price/Size	Purchase Price/Size	Purchase Price/Size
Invl/Company if any	Invl/Company if any	Invl/Company if any
Alcohol cost Per Ounce	Alcohol cost Per Ounce	Alcohol cost Per Ounce
# Ounces Used	# Ounces Used	# Ounces Used
Cost of This Alcohol	Cost of This Alcohol	Cost of This Alcohol
Additive #1	Additive #2	Additive #3
Company Name	Company Name	Company Name
Company Address	Company Address	Company Address
Company Phone	Company Phone	Company Phone
Inv #	Inv #	Inv #
Amt Purchased	Amt Purchased	Amt Purchased
Amount Used	Amount Used	Amount Used
Cost of Additive	Cost of Additive	Cost of Additive
Bottles	Labels	Packaging
Company Name	Company Name	Company Name
Company Address	Company Address	Company Address
Company Phone	Company Phone	Company Phone
Inv #	Inv #	Inv #
Amt Purchased	Amt Purchased	Amt Purchased
Amount Used	Amount Used	Amount Used
Cost of Bottles	Cost of labels per batch	Cost of pkging per batch

Batch

Batch Name

Total Cost of Beans	
Total Ounces of Beans	
Total # beans used	
Average Per Bean Cost	
Total Cost of Alcohol Used	
Total Ounces of Alcohol Used	
Average Per oz cost of Alcohol	
Total Cost of Additives Used	
Total Bottle Cost	
Total Label Cost	
Total Packaging Cost	
Misc Fees	
Misc Fees	
Total Misc Fees	
Total Cost of this Batch	
Total Ounces in thes Batch	
Total Cost per Ounce	
Sale Price per Ounce	
Profit per ounce	

Batch Rating

	1	2	3	4	5	6	7	8	9	10
Bean Rating	1	2	3	4	5	6	7	8	9	10
Alcohol Rating	1	2	3	4	5	6	7	8	9	10
Final Rating	1	2	3	4	5	6	7	8	9	10
Customer Rating	1	2	3	4	5	6	7	8	9	10

Batch Preparation Notes

Batch Diary by Date

Simple Vanilla Recipe

Born on Date _____ Strain Date _____

Bottle Date _____ Finished ounces _____

Recipe Name _____

Alcohol #1 _____ Oz. _____

Alcohol #2 _____ Oz. _____

Alcohol #3 _____ Oz. _____

Alcohol #4 _____ Oz. _____

Alcohol #5 _____ Oz. _____

Bean Brand _____

Ounces used _____

Additives #1 _____Date added _____

Additives #2 _____Date added _____

Notes _____

_____

_____

Batch

Batch Name

Column 1	Column 2	Column 3
Born on Date	Fold Strength	(B-A) Ratio oz ml
	Strained Date if any	Date Finished
Bean Name #1	Bean Name #2	Bean Name #3
Bean Company	Bean Company	Bean Company
Invoice Number	Invoice Number	Invoice Number
Company Address/Origin	Company Address/Origin	Company Address/Origin
Company Phone #	Company Phone #	Company Phone #
or Purchased From	or Purchased From	or Purchased From
Purchase Date/ Arrival Date	Purchase Date/ Arrival Date	Purchase Date/ Arrival Date
Bean Grade/Length	Bean Grade/Length	Bean Grade/Length
Ounces of Beans	Ounces of Beans	Ounces of Beans
Number of Beans per Ounce	Number of Beans per Ounce	Number of Beans per Ounce
Per Bean Cost	Per Bean Cost	Per Bean Cost
Total Cost This Bean/Recipe	Total Cost This Bean/Recipe	Total Cost This Bean/Recipe
Alcohol #1 Name	Alcohol #2 Name	Alcohol #3 Name
Proof	Proof	Proof
Purchase Price/Size	Purchase Price/Size	Purchase Price/Size
Invl/Company if any	Invl/Company if any	Invl/Company if any
Alcohol cost Per Ounce	Alcohol cost Per Ounce	Alcohol cost Per Ounce
# Ounces Used	# Ounces Used	# Ounces Used
Cost of This Alcohol	Cost of This Alcohol	Cost of This Alcohol
Alcohol #4 Name	Alcohol #5 Name	Alcohol #6 Name
Proof	Proof	Proof
Purchase Price/Size	Purchase Price/Size	Purchase Price/Size
Invl/Company if any	Invl/Company if any	Invl/Company if any
Alcohol cost Per Ounce	Alcohol cost Per Ounce	Alcohol cost Per Ounce
# Ounces Used	# Ounces Used	# Ounces Used
Cost of This Alcohol	Cost of This Alcohol	Cost of This Alcohol
Additive #1	Additive #2	Additive #3
Company Name	Company Name	Company Name
Company Address	Company Address	Company Address
Company Phone	Company Phone	Company Phone
Inv #	Inv #	Inv #
Amt Purchased	Amt Purchased	Amt Purchased
Amount Used	Amount Used	Amount Used
Cost of Additive	Cost of Additive	Cost of Additive
Bottles	Labels	Packaging
Company Name	Company Name	Company Name
Company Address	Company Address	Company Address
Company Phone	Company Phone	Company Phone
Inv #	Inv #	Inv #
Amt Purchased	Amt Purchased	Amt Purchased
Amount Used	Amount Used	Amount Used
Cost of Bottles	Cost of labels per batch	Cost of pkging per batch

Batch #   Batch Name

		Batch Rating										
Total Cost of Beans												
Total Ounces of Beans		Bean Rating	1	2	3	4	5	6	7	8	9	10
Total # beans used		Alcohol Rating	1	2	3	4	5	6	7	8	9	10
Average Per Bean Cost		Final Rating	1	2	3	4	5	6	7	8	9	10
Total Cost of Alcohol Used		Customer Rating	1	2	3	4	5	6	7	8	9	10
Total Ounces of Alcohol Used												
Average Per oz cost of Alcohol												
Total Cost of Additives Used												
Total Bottle Cost												
Total Label Cost												
Total Packaging Cost												
Misc Fees												
Misc Fees												
Total Mist Fees												
Total Cost of this Batch												
Total Ounces in thes Batch												
Total Cost per Ounce												
Sale Price per Ounce												
Profit per ounce												

Batch Preparation Notes

Batch Diary by Date

Notes

Notes

Notes

I'd like to thank my friend Deanne for helping me with this book and the wonderful people at Madagascar Vanilla Company for never letting me down!

Printed in Great Britain
by Amazon

21611662R00058